Praise for *Above t*

T0268363

If you're searching for insights into how to lead with your values in a way that makes a lasting difference, Arkadi Kuhlmann's *Above the Clouds* is an informative, engaging, and easy-to-apply toolkit for leadership in a digital era.
— SENATOR CHRIS COONS, Delaware

Arkadi Kuhlmann's investigation of culture and leadership is at once practical, accessible, and coherent. Never preachy, Kuhlmann allows would-be leaders to discover their own callings and provides a helpful road map on how to build a durable culture that reflects their own reality. Bravo.
— JOHN GIBSON, CEO, Integral Capital Partners

Many people talk about culture and leadership — Arkadi lives it, understands it, and can teach it.
— BILL HARRIS, founder, Evergreen Money; former CEO, PayPal, Intuit, and Personal Finance

In this compelling read, Arkadi Kuhlmann shares his leadership lessons focused on culture-driven leadership and why it is vital to success. As they say, "Culture eats strategy for breakfast," and great leaders do get culture right.
— JON LOVE, executive chair and founder, KingSett Capital

Focusing on the customer, valuing employees, and taking time to reflect, instead of reacting, are just a few of the many nuggets of wisdom found in *Above the Clouds*, which will help you take a different leadership perspective.
— DICKSON L. LOUIE, lecturer, Graduate School of Management, University of California, Davis, and board member, the Robert C. Maynard Institute for Journalism Education

Above the Clouds is a book on leadership, specifically culture-driven leadership. Arkadi Kuhlmann takes his readers through the essence of culture-driven leadership by citing many examples from his own entrepreneurial and innovative career as well as relying on many of the roads travelled by other well-known CEOs. He tells it the way it really is — he has been there. A thoughtful book for any aspiring leader.

— PIERRE L. MORRISSETTE, executive chairman, Pelmorex Corp.

Arkadi hits the mark again with his latest book on culture. An authentic organizational purpose is critical to attracting talent and in aligning what a firm does to what it wants to achieve. Strategy and culture are how a firm bridges that gap. Both are required for success. In this book, Arkadi Kuhlmann challenges the reader to define the kind of leader they will be (or are) and to question if culture-driven leadership is the better avenue for them to embrace. In my work with thousands of entrepreneurs over the years I'm convinced that it is.

— ERIC A. MORSE, PH.D., Morrissette chair in entrepreneurship, executive director, Morrissette Institute for Entrepreneurship, Western University

Getting "above the clouds" to see the landscape in a holistic way has never been more challenging for business leaders, given the fast pace of change and challenges in our global society. Drawing on his own journey, Arkadi Kuhlmann shows how culture-driven leadership can create and maintain a consistent narrative that keeps organizations on the right path, leads people to achieve excellence, and enables that broader vision to stay in focus.

— ALAN SHEPARD, president and vice-chancellor, Western University

ABOVE THE CLOUDS

ABOVE THE CLOUDS

Rediscovering the Power of Culture-Driven Leadership

ARKADI KUHLMANN

DUNDURN
PRESS

Publisher: Meghan Macdonald | Acquiring editor: Kwame Scott Fraser | Editor: Dominic Farrell
Cover designer: Laura Boyle
Cover image: istock.com/Benjamin Toth

Library and Archives Canada Cataloguing in Publication

Title: Above the clouds : rediscovering the power of culture-driven leadership / Arkadi Kuhlmann.
Names: Kuhlmann, Arkadi, 1946- author.
Description: Includes bibliographical references.
Identifiers: Canadiana (print) 20240369416 | Canadiana (ebook) 20240369459 | ISBN 9781459754621 (softcover) | ISBN 9781459754638 (PDF) | ISBN 9781459754645 (EPUB)
Subjects: LCSH: Leadership.
Classification: LCC HD57.7 .K84 2024 | DDC 658.4/092—dc23

We acknowledge the support of the Canada Council for the Arts and the Ontario Arts Council for our publishing program. We also acknowledge the financial support of the Government of Ontario, through the Ontario Book Publishing Tax Credit and Ontario Creates, and the Government of Canada.

Printed and bound in Canada.

Dundurn Press
1382 Queen Street East
Toronto, Ontario, Canada M4L 1C9
dundurn.com, @dundurnpress

This book is dedicated to the alumni of ING Direct and Zenbanx, who continue to lead the way in the creation of a valuable customer experience.

CONTENTS

Introduction

WE NEED (BETTER) LEADERSHIP MORE THAN EVER

Why culture-driven leadership?

Simple: it works. And it works much better over time than the alternative, which I am defining as context-driven leadership. Context-driven leadership is defensive in nature and directed at mostly short-term outcomes. Why is time important? A recent study reported in *Barron's* annual Top CEOs issue concluded that "the median tenure among the S&P 500 companies" was less than five years.[1] Ten years ago the average was more than seven years. And unfortunately, tenures continue to shrink. A CEO with ambition and big plans likely won't have a lot of time to lead a company to greater success.

It would seem to make sense, therefore, for a CEO to focus on short-term goals and achieve success in the limited timeframe allotted them. It turns out that's not a good route to take. The argument in this book is that culture-driven leadership is the only viable option that will deal effectively with those shorter and shorter timeframes. In other words, culture-driven leadership can address complexity better. How do I know this? Personal experience. This book isn't about me, however. It's about leaders of the future. Who will they be? What will they need to know? Most important: Are you one of them?

. . .

Whenever I think about culture — what it means — I recall a meeting back in the early 2000s, when I was in the process of securing a location for the new ING Direct USA corporate offices in Wilmington, Delaware. My Dutch investors expected me to select a more conventional location, like New York or Boston. Not only was Wilmington not a traditional banking centre, it was home to the biggest credit card companies. What in the world was an upstart internet savings bank doing there? "That's just the point," I said. "What better place to be the David to the industry Goliath?"

They came out for a visit. I was worried, of course, they'd decide I was in over my head, but by the end of the visit, they had bought into my strategy, which boiled down to this: *Why take a conventional approach to building a business that is all about breaking the rules?* When I explained my thinking, the chairman pulled me aside. He wanted me to know that he liked my plan and added that I was the only American he could trust.

I thanked him but didn't have the heart to tell him the truth. "I'm Canadian." It was for me a classic and incredibly illuminating leadership moment that I have never forgotten. Know who you are; even better, know who others assume you are.

. . .

I am a passionate advocate of culture-driven leadership. I think that leadership is more important than ever — but not just any kind of leadership. Over the course of the book, I hope it will become clear why culture-driven leadership is the most effective kind of leadership, the kind most likely to ensure the sustained success of a company or organization.

Our need for talented leadership is one of the biggest challenges we face in the decade ahead. Not long ago, I received a call from a friend and colleague. A respected and extremely talented administrator and academic at a prestigious business school, he wanted me to know he was turning down an opportunity to extend his contract. Naturally, I was stunned. I asked him why. He told me that he felt that he was increasingly having to fight what was a "no win" battle. Every day he was faced with a new test he had to pass; the energy that he would have preferred to spend on the exciting and important leadership challenges of planning for the future was being sucked up by having to mediate the endless squabbling of rival factions. Frankly, it wasn't the first time I had heard a leadership colleague expressing serious doubts — not about leadership but *the possibility* of leadership.

I've spent the largest part of my career as a passionate advocate on behalf of culture-driven leadership. It's a position that was unusual early on in my career, but not anymore. Today, you can stumble across a reference to it on almost an hourly basis. An online search I made recently for "business culture articles" turned up about 835 million results; there were about the same number on "corporate culture." Unfortunately for me, I also found 3.7 million references to *books* about business culture. Why another? I wrote this book for two reasons: first, to discuss the unprecedented challenges businesses face today; and second, to review again why culture-driven leadership will be such a valuable tool in meeting those challenges.

WHAT'S IN A NAME?

When you hear the name Elon Musk, what immediately comes to mind? How about Richard Branson? Both are incredibly successful and well-known entrepreneurs and CEOs. But that's about all they have in common. It isn't just that they have different styles. It's more than that. They each, through what they say and do, generate a different kind of culture; they live differently. And that difference is reflected in the very different cultures that they have created in the companies that they run. These two very different men drive very different corporate cultures.

The *Merriam-Webster Dictionary* defines culture as "the customary beliefs, social forms, and material traits of a racial, religious, or social group; also: the characteristic features of everyday existence (such as diversions or a way of life) shared by people in a place or time."*

---

* See Appendix A for a fuller discussion.

"Some workers," a business journal suggested, think "[culture] is a sense of organizational belonging and a strong connection to colleagues. Others say it is a set of shared values and beliefs that guide decisions. Some define it as an intangible asset described as the soul of the company."[2] However it is defined, workers have made it clear that they believe culture plays a major role in a company's success. The problem business leaders face today is that culture means different things to different people. Creating a consensus or finding common ground is harder and harder. It is up to leaders to define that culture. I believe that the success of a business depends to a huge degree on harnessing the power of culture-driven leadership. To that end, it will be helpful to think of culture as "how" we get things done as a priority, not just what we get done.

OUR BRAVE NEW WORLD

We hear a lot about *inclusion*. Welcoming and valuing everyone is import-ant; we all benefit. Practising inclusion is the right thing to do. The paradox of modern life, however, is that as society recognizes diversity and becomes more inclusive,* we are also becoming more divided. It is getting harder to figure out what we have in common. Culture-driven leadership is focused on finding commonalities, shared interests, and aspirations. It's not where we're from that matters, right? It's where we want to go. That's the heart and soul of culture-driven leadership.

Trust in traditional institutions — government, courts, the media, uni-versities, law enforcement, religion, and so on — has dropped to the lowest levels ever. In a U.S. study, people described their society as "struggling," "negative," "lost," and "bad," and described their country as "[going] down-hill, divided." They found themselves "doubting democracy, falling behind, and tuning out."[3] Experts tell us that, overall, we have never been better off, but privately, we feel that the opposite is true. Familiar traditions and

---

* As concepts, "diversity" and "inclusion" would seem antithetical in nature, which is perhaps at least one source of contemporary confusion about what normative behaviour is supposed to be. Respecting diversity while at the same time being inclusive presents a tricky challenge for a leader who is responsible for defining the tribe (another name for the culture). "Who am I?" and "Where do I (we) belong?"

forms of authority are being attacked. Polls tell us that young people have little faith in the ability of capitalism to improve their lives, don't feel that optimistic about the future, and have no belief that anything of value can be learned from the past. We live in a world that many see as meaningless, where there is what one historian described as an "erosion of inherited beliefs and customs."[4]

We can't express an opinion, idea, preference, or observation, or register a disagreement, without the worry that having done so we will be branded, shamed, humiliated, harassed, ostracized, or "cancelled." Years ago, it was generally accepted that conflicts could be resolved through dialogue, that if we could only get to the root of our disagreements, we would realize we have more in common than what separates us. That idea seems naive today. According to a recent Pew Research study, only 55 percent of Americans have "a great deal or even a fair amount of confidence in their fellow Americans when it comes to making judgments ... about issues facing the country." In other words, we don't trust our leaders, and don't trust one another, either. Who's left? And what does that mean for society?

Interestingly, those polled identified business as "the most trusted institution in the country at present."[5] In fact, business ranked higher than government when people were asked to state which institutions had the competencies required to effect meaningful social change, and higher when it comes to ethics overall.* That's the good news. The not-so-good news is that most also believe that business is not doing enough at present "to address the larger issues that are facing the world." Those polled stated that business needs to be even "more engaged." A huge majority of consumers (87 percent) said they'd "purchase a product because a company advocated for an issue they cared about," and "more than 75 percent *would refuse* to purchase a product if they found out a company supported an issue contrary to their beliefs."[6]

According to a report by the World Economic Forum, "business leaders are facing new and difficult challenges, and ... an ecology that is evolving

---

* No doubt this explains why business news has muscled its way onto the front pages and has made odd (and even notorious) celebrities of entrepreneurs like Elon Musk, Jeff Bezos, and Mark Zuckerberg. Musk, for instance, has one hundred million followers on X.

rapidly … in ways that are hard to predict and even harder to manage."[7] And there are other new problems facing leaders. The Covid-19 pandemic, for instance, virtually overnight became the greatest economic challenge since the Great Depression. It created social and cultural challenges, too, which in turn put (and continue to put) enormous pressure on leaders to successfully navigate new and unfamiliar terrain.

An unexpected consequence of the pandemic and the sudden global shutdown of huge sectors of the economy was that an unprecedented number of workers had time to re-evaluate their employment situation, goals, needs, preferences, and long-term prospects, and millions decided to leave the workforce in an out-of-market migration known as the Great Resignation. Suffice to say, no one saw this coming, and no one really knows where we are headed.

Currently, businesses in many sectors are struggling not only with finding employees to fill positions but finding the right employees. As a result, many businesses are experiencing what has been termed a "skills deficit." One major driver of this migration, according to the report, "appears to be that many workers are no longer willing to put up with the pay and/or working conditions they accepted before the pandemic."[8] Indeed, the summary of the federal government's final jobs report in 2022 concluded as much: it's hard to find enough workers for some jobs. In the 1930s, the problem was millions of workers looking for jobs (any job), while today, it's millions of open jobs with too few workers.

In a segment about the job situation that appeared on the *PBS NewsHour* in January 2023, the correspondent suggested a generational explanation for the deficit: "young people just aren't interested."[9] They have, it was suggested, a different work ethic than older generations. When a twenty-something was asked about what she needed from a job, she answered, "[I would only take a job] if I knew that my labor would be valued, that my personhood would be valued, that I wouldn't just be another cog in this machine that keeps endlessly grinding us downwards."[10] Today, workers wish to play a larger role in deciding what a company's culture will be, which is creating formidable challenges for leaders engaged in long-term planning and establishing goals.

That leadership is always adapting to new contexts and conditions is not news; flexibility is needed. But how flexible can leadership be before it ceases being leadership? The world is not merely changing generationally; the changes are structural and foundational. What that will mean for leaders and for leadership is not at all clear. Is meaningful leadership — are leaders — on the endangered species list? How will young leaders learn what they need to know about leadership to thrive? After all, we all benefit from effective and meaningful leadership. And maybe you think you might be a leader who will end up making a difference.

Are we ready? Are *you* ready?

HOW CHANGE HAPPENS

I am a member of a generation that well remembers President John F. Kennedy inspiring a nation to find in itself — inside each and every citizen — the hidden or unexploited resources of leadership for creating a better America and a better world. "Ask not what your country can do for you — ask what you can do for your country." Or, as I like to say, *Change won't happen until someone wants it to happen.*

Effective leadership requires the setting of priorities. Tell me what you pay attention to, and I will tell you who you are, in other words.[11] What are you paying attention to? What are you focused on? What is the commitment you are making? We'll consider these things in detail in the chapters that follow, but for now, remember that how a leader answers questions like these will make all the difference. As I hope will become clear in the pages ahead, the power of *culture-driven* leadership requires a deep understanding of a culture. Step one: rethink what *we think* we know about culture. Only when we've done that can we create the culture we need. What is it? How do we recognize it? What changes culture? How is it sustained? How do I use it to drive my leadership for the desired outcome?

WHY CULTURE IS SO IMPORTANT*

Shaping a culture is a formidable task. Only the best leaders can accomplish that feat. Emotional maturity, authenticity, and a strong character are all essential leadership qualities, and all are crucial to successfully lead a culture-driven company. Unfortunately, these and other valuable qualities needed to be a great leader are not taught in a classroom. They can be developed, but only life can provide the necessary lessons.

Also essential is an alignment between the leader's passion, the company's mission, and the corporate culture in which everything transpires. To have an impact in this new environment, a leader's ethos must be closely aligned with the culture of the company they hope to lead. Aspects of that culture might be particular to that corporation, but it's also likely that the culture as a whole is reflective of a much broader culture, reflecting the language and nationality, or ages and interests, of the employees. A leader whose own culture is in step with a company's culture is likely to be much more effective. The most important question to ask about corporate culture is whether workers think they're in a job — or on a mission. A visionary leader is on a mission and inspires their employees to feel that way, too.

ARE YOU A CULTURE-DRIVEN LEADER?

Do you have what it takes? A culture-driven leader will possess the following six fundamental attributes.

1. **A calling:** What's your cause?
2. **The guts to make the calling personal:** Your mission must come from a real place. Otherwise, authenticity is missing, and no one sees the leader "walking the talk." The leader can't be an invention of the marketing department or someone who mouths carefully scripted talking points. The leader has to be the author of the mission and feel a passion for it.

---

* See Appendix A for a fuller discussion.

3. **A talent for identifying the powerful enemy that needs defeating:** If there's no one to fight, there's no job for the white knight. For ING Direct, credit card companies that pushed spending with no consideration for the costs to the consumer were the enemy. The defeat of a dark force is a highly effective leadership goal. The thought or image of an enemy transforms competitors into dragons to be slain by all employees. You believe that you are one of the "good guys." For workers, this makes coming to work every day more heroic and more of an adventure.

4. **An ability to choose a superior inner circle:** Picking a core team is one of a leader's most fundamental responsibilities. Unfortunately, it's not easy to find and select people who are willing and able to join a mission. A gift for spotting talent is hugely important. The normal recruitment process does not work, and you're not likely going to find the right person among the contacts of your colleagues. Ironically, it's not unusual to find just who you need in an unusual place. Character and motivation are the two qualities that separate loyal, enthusiastic workers from mere jobholders. Most people can put together a good-looking curriculum vitae. Often, though, the best hire is someone who has experienced failure and has something to prove to themselves and the world.

5. **The ability to deal with the possibility of failure:** Working in a constant state of imminent crisis is not for the faint of heart. Anxiety can result from a company-wide sense that the organization and everyone in it are potential prey for an outside force. However, without the risk of failure, there is a danger that everyone will grow complacent; corporate overconfidence can become the silent killer. A sense of crisis keeps the enterprise in an energetic, startup frame of mind.

6. **An aura of mystery:** A leader can't make things appear too mechanical. To drive the passion of your company,

you have to create some mystery around you. You need to appear in some small way different from those that look to you. Team members want to follow, but they need a reason to do so. Your leadership has to work like pixie dust.

I said you needed a cause. What does that mean? Your "why" and the company mission statement need to align. An effective vision has to be one that shakes up the status quo and starts a revolution. No one will ever be inspired by a puddle of ambiguity. Too many corporate mission statements are diluted into dullness by a requirement to obtain consensus and the demand for multiple levels of approval, making them utterly ineffective for rallying the troops. A mission statement is the best leadership tool you can ever invent. In grassroots political organizations, the sense of being on a mission develops almost spontaneously, without central leadership, because enough people believe in the cause. A team with a purpose beats a team with a process any day.

So what makes the difference between a forgettable mission statement and one that turns workers into devotees? There are five key qualities to consider.

1. A mission statement must advocate for someone. Who are you fighting for?
2. The goal in the mission statement should be nearly impossible to achieve. Reaching for the goal is the inspiring and satisfying part. It's a journey. The horizon should always remain just out of reach.
3. A mission statement should read like poetry. It should be sonorous and simple, and catchy enough that people won't be able to get it out of their heads.
4. A mission statement should be written with the leader and the most loyal followers in mind. It should not try to please everyone. It has to matter to the people who show up every day.
5. The mission statement must come from the top. Defining the company's purpose is a leader's responsibility. Committees might be good for many things, but not when it comes to

leadership. The leader is responsible for defining the company's cause and must embody it.

WHY "ABOVE THE CLOUDS"?

The trip had been a disaster. Not only was I convinced we had made no progress, I left for the airport convinced the project was dead. I am never good with failure. I take it personally, so this was hard to take. At the airport, I was like a zombie. The events of the day just kept replaying in my head: Why did it go this way and not that way? What did I do wrong? What should I have done differently? Thoughts just kept churning round and round in my head; the noise was deafening.

Suddenly, it was like a switch had flipped. The noise in my head cleared. I was looking out the window, thousands of feet above the ground. I marvelled at the view, at how "right" everything looked. Sky, clouds, plains, mountains, rivers, cities, towns, roads and highways like spidery veins. It all seemed to work. No chaos or confusion, nothing out of order; everything seemed to fit together exactly as it was meant to. On the ground, I knew that was not the case. Such a simple and even everyday insight, but it brought an incredible and much-needed perspective, as well as a sense of calm. Spending time above the clouds made all the difference.

Let me explain. What I see more and more today is leaders paying lip service to the importance of culture — just another means to an end. It should be (and can be) much more. As we all know, the world is changing at a rate that makes it impossible to keep up; for a leader charged with navigating life in the crowded fast lane of global change, the white-knuckle pace can be challenging and intimidating. Even the best and most accomplished leaders (as we will see) can find themselves at the top of the ladder one day and roadkill the next. It's the right time, I believe, to revisit the idea of culture-driven leadership — the right time to rediscover its power. The motivational plaque on the wall is nice but it probably doesn't have much impact.

GETTING STARTED

In *Above the Clouds*, I address myself to exploring the open questions and challenges faced by culture-driven leadership today. The book will be, I hope, a dialogue with young entrepreneurs or aspiring executives — to anyone anywhere and in any walk of life who has ever wondered if they have leadership skills or potential.

This is not a "how do I become a leader" book. It's more an ongoing "no right answer" discussion about discovering who you want to be as a leader. What *kind* of leader do you want to be? The challenges a leader faces change over time. What will that mean for you? Critically, what is it about leadership that stays the same?

Remaining true to a goal despite changing challenges is what defines *culture*-driven leadership. Redefining goals when faced with changing challenges is what defines *context*-driven leadership. Context here refers to the specific set of circumstances, conditions, and issues that exist or prevail within or act on a company at any given time. Culture is a set of behaviours or principles that prevails and remains steady across a series of different contexts. For instance, a company culture that traditionally has prioritized "friendly," quality customer service might be threatened by changes made by a leader brought in to cut costs during difficult times.

The chapters are loosely themed around the ten principles that have structured my culture-driven leadership career. I hope they work for you. You may come up with your own set based on your own sense of what matters and is most important to you as a leader. I've steered clear of technical jargon; the tone is conversational, and the arrangement is exploratory. The chapters are numbered, but my hope is that you'll feel free to jump back and forth between them, agreeing or disagreeing, and pushing the conversation. I don't pretend to have all the answers. I do have a lot of questions. In fact, I am unapologetically Socratic in my conviction that asking questions is the best way to spark and build productive debate. Anyone who has spent time in the learning forum of case studies will see this pedagogy here. This book, in other words, is a way to help you find the leader inside you. As I said, the world needs leaders today more than ever. That leader could be anyone. You could be from anywhere, from any background, from any walk of life.

Who knows, you could even be a Canadian!

ACTION POINTS

I've distilled my experience with culture-driven leadership into the
following nine "boot camp" basics about culture. This list is neither
exhaustive nor carved in stone. Let it serve as a starting point for
your own exploration of what culture means to you and your own
leadership style.

- Every company has a culture. Does the company have the culture it needs? As a leader, you need to know if you have what it takes to create and sustain the right culture at the right time.
- The task of any leader is to always be identifying culture. Culture is never static. It is always changing, always evolving. Since culture is the sum of beliefs, behaviours, assumptions, conventions, innovations, habits, biases, values, and prejudices that exist in a company, the leader is responsible for answering the question, "Who are we?"
- Culture does not always identify itself.
- Effective culture-driven leadership requires that culture be identified. "How are things done here?"
- "What is acceptable?" A leader needs to know what boundaries exist, and why.
- "Are you one of us?" We should identify with a culture (and with its trajectory). Dissent weakens culture. Culture should promote a powerful desire for membership and belonging.
- Personal traits are strong cultural filters. Never assume everyone understands the culture in the same way.
- Only the truth works in culture.
- Actions count more than words. Be the culture you expect from others.

THE PRINCIPLES

Rock Then Roll laid out the principles that ING Direct used to guide its business and manage its growth. They've been updated a bit to even better meet the challenges of a globalized economy. It's the best starting point for building a team and building the existing business. The principles are as follows:

1. We are new here.
2. We are here to create, not destroy.
3. We will constantly learn.
4. We will listen; we will simplify.
5. We will be fair.
6. We will tell the truth.
7. We will be for everyone.
8. Our mission is to help improve lives.
9. We will never stop asking why.
10. We will never be finished.

CAVEAT EMPTOR

By way of warning, when you read the principles outlined in the chapter headings, you may think that they sound too simple and generic. I know all this, you may think. None of this is new. And you would be right. Nothing you will read will be alien or unknown. We all — each one of us — already have a familiarity with and understanding of principles that we use as guides. They are our values and beliefs. An "above the clouds" perspective entails taking the long-term consequences of action into account. It keeps culture-driven leadership relevant, not just in the short term but the long term.

Opening Thought

CULTURE VERSUS CONTEXT

I have only to stamp my foot upon the ground, and there will rise up armies of infantry and armies of cavalry.

— Pompey on the threat to Rome posed by Julius Caesar

Business students are familiar with case studies. It's how we condense and present real-life business challenges in the classroom, the idea obviously being that simulated exercises will better prepare students for real life. As a student and a professor, I have been on both sides of the lectern. What I can say is this: no matter how "real" the classroom experience is, it isn't.

A lesson from history might help illustrate.

Two figures are engaged in battle. On one side is Gnaeus Pompeius Magnus, military hero and ally of Rome's senatorial elite. On the other stands Julius Caesar, another famous military hero, a former ally of Pompey, an aristocrat, but also, nominally, the people's defender. At stake: the fate of Rome and the republic. The year: 48 BC.

The outcome of the contest seemed a foregone conclusion. Caesar's army was exiled far from home, starving, completely cut off from supplies, and vastly outnumbered. Pompey, meanwhile, enjoyed not only numerical superiority but also the full backing and plentiful resources of the powerful anti-Caesar faction in the Senate. (It was, in fact, Pompey family money that had built the Senate house in which the senators plotted Caesar's downfall after labelling him as an "enemy of Rome.")

Pompey's victory appeared assured. In an earlier engagement, in fact, Pompey's army had routed Caesar's forces, but instead of pressing his advantage and wiping out Caesar and his army once and for all — as his senatorial colleagues had expected — he inexplicably disengaged, allowing Caesar and his army to withdraw into the mountainous interior of Greece. The Senate was apoplectic; impatient anti-Caesarians turned their displeasure on Pompey, questioning his decision-making, his tactics, his advanced age, his competence, his timid leadership, even his manliness and courage.*

In turn, Pompey, outraged and offended (understandably), turned his wrath on the Senate, sneering at their "soft metropolitan manners"[1] and what five-star Pentagon generals today would dismiss as carping complaints from politicians who were nothing but "desk jockey" warriors and effete, paper-pushing bureaucrats.

Unfortunately, as a historian has written, the value he put on the opinion of the senatorial establishment was Pompey's one critical weakness. It would be the cause of his ignominious undoing. Pompey lost effectiveness as a leader when he allowed himself to become distracted by political rather than military objectives.

Pompey — as Caesar had anticipated — unwisely goaded into action by the torrent of criticism and trusting as decisive his numerical superiority, engaged Caesar at a place called Pharsalus. At first, all went well for Pompey. Caesar, however, had kept in reserve a seasoned elite element of his cavalry, which, having lured Pompey's army into a trap, he would unleash. He instructed his soldiers to strike with their javelins upwards and into the faces of their enemy.

---

* At the very least, this should be a lesson in how leadership has not and will never change: those who lead will always be targets of criticism for those who don't. It's a lesson any effective leader needs to learn. It's not a pretty picture, but when it comes to human nature, we tend to take out more than we want to put in. It's a fact of life with many profound and/or everyday consequences; leaders need to understand human nature. They cannot ignore it. The graveyards are full of failed idealists. Leadership means getting it done. Human nature is context.

"It was a moment of military genius," a historian has written.[2] Caesar guessed correctly that Pompey's soldiers, comprised mainly of "the flower of Rome's aristocratic youth … had neither the experience nor the stomach" for combat of such raw fierceness and violence. Pompey's troops suddenly found themselves backtracking in terrified disarray as Caesar's rampaging cavalry flew at their unprotected flanks. It was a historic victory in which Caesar triumphed over an army with vastly superior numbers, resources, and tactical support.

As we know, however, the story did not end with Caesar's triumph. A short four years later, Caesar was ousted — assassinated on the floor of the Senate — in what may have been the most brutal board of directors meeting in history. It seems that he wasn't genuinely interested in "reforming the republic," as he had promised, "and building relationships with the Senate." Rather, it appears that Caesar "ultimately cared more about his patrician dignity and honours accorded it than the liberty of the people." In trying to gain complete power over the affairs of Rome via a military coup, Caesar alienated the political establishment whose support he needed to effectively govern.

Two very different leaders, but two similar results. Pompey lost effectiveness as a leader when he allowed himself to become distracted by political rather than military objectives. By demanding complete power over the affairs of Rome via a military coup, Caesar, on the other hand, committed the opposite mistake: alienating the political establishment he needed to effectively govern. Why is this important? What could any of this mean for leaders of today? Pompey and Caesar failed what I will be calling the leadership context challenge. Pompey vastly exaggerated his capacity for commanding context. "I have only to stamp my foot!" he boasted of his ability to dominate events. Meanwhile, Caesar, without a serious rival, failed to make the many reforms demanded by the people that, for their support, he had promised to enact. As we might conclude today, in his corporate quest for power, he lost touch with both the brand and the customer, so much so that when the biggest threat to his leadership arrived, he did not see it coming, *not until it was too late.*

Both generals — each in his own way — failed the culture-driven leadership challenge. We'll consider other examples of successes and failures in the chapters ahead. Just remember: *successful* leadership is never guaranteed.

THE LEADERSHIP CONTEXT

The nineteenth-century English philosopher Herbert Spencer famously defined life as "the continuous adjustment of internal relations to external relations," which is a neat way of zeroing in on the culture/context dynamic. A crucially important point to keep in mind moving forward is that culture and context are linked but are not the same. What Spencer called "external relations" are just what we mean by the challenges leaders face every day. It's the context in which they operate. For instance, Caesar mastered the military context but flubbed the political; Pompey, on the other hand, aligned himself with the political but not the military.

Using Spencer's terminology, culture-driven leadership ensures that the adjustments in internal relations necessary to respond to changes in external relations (changing contexts) will always align with meeting the goals of the values- or principles-based reference system (culture). It's unlikely that there will always be perfect alignment, of course. Nothing is ever perfect. But the results will be better and more reliable than adjustments made with no reference to the culture.

As we move along in the book, I will be introducing leadership insights and concepts that have been foundational in my career. Leadership is never as simple and straightforward as it might appear to those who don't practise it. Case studies are hugely valuable. But figuring out what to do when you are "at the controls" and the outcome is unknown cannot be learned *at a distance*. We do what we can to prepare, but nothing can compare to *being there*. Your actual experiences will be different (context is never the same), but the functional role of leadership doesn't change. The idea behind these leadership insights is to distinguish what endures (culture) from what is temporary (context). Context-focused leadership can thrive for a brief span of time but will falter with a shift of context. Leadership driven by culture, however, can navigate through changes of context.

Again, it isn't vital that you agree with me. What's important is deciding what matters to you and how you see yourself evolving into the leadership role you want. That doesn't happen overnight. The leadership path doesn't run from A to B. And once you're at the top, the job has only just begun. For one thing, it's incredibly lonely at the top. Are you prepared for that? Most of us are okay with success, but what about failure? The buck stops with you! There's no one to turn to when the outcome is in the balance. You're it! Did you get it right? Or wrong? It's how you'll be judged.*

---

* An important contention of this book is that context — specifically the nature of context to be changing constantly — means 1) that more decisions are being required and 2) the probability of making the wrong decision is increasing. Even more problematic is how we define "wrong." A decision that makes perfect business sense in one context can be disastrous in another, as we will see.

Chapter 1

WE ARE NEW HERE

It's a point of view and a state of mind. Yesterday is over; today is a new day. Take what lessons can be learned and move on. Face every day with fresh eyes and a mind open to new opportunities. Keep looking ahead; be inquisitive; keep wondering "how?" How can we do better for our customer? Not for ourselves or our bottom line, but for the customer. This takes commitment, discipline, and focus. It also requires humility. Enjoy your success, but with moderation. Easy to say, hard to do, really. It demands working every day with a new sense of tomorrow, but it drives growth and refreshes a sensibility for opportunity. An effective leader who embodies the "we are new here" ethos will be an inspiration for others to do the same.

• • •

"We are new here" was the principle at the heart of ING Direct's culture. Established in Canada in 1997, the bank had no branches. That was the idea. Instead, all activity was transacted using 1-800 numbers or through the internet.* Customers initially called up to open their accounts and would mail their first deposit by cheque.

---

* We will examine the "1-800 number problem" shortly.

To keep it simple (for the customer *and* us), we offered only one product: a savings account that paid the same high interest rate on all accounts. What about fees or hidden charges? None. What if someone opened a bigger account? Shouldn't they get a better rate? Nope. It was the same rate for everyone, no matter who you were. And as for fine print. There wasn't any. It was a one-product offer with one rate. No monthly statements mailed out. No exceptions.

No other bank was doing it, and no other bank was taking seriously the idea that banking could be done any other way but their *established way*. We wanted to prove them wrong. And we did.[*]

Fundamental to the business was the mindset that it's all about enhancing the *overall* customer experience (from first contact to delivery and beyond). It doesn't mean much if you think it's new and different; what's important is what your customer thinks. Where is *their* buy-in? And are you doing everything in your power to make sure they stay bought-in?

Since most of our business was going to be conducted over the phone, we knew that we had to show that when our customers called us their experience would be different from what they were used to when they called other businesses. We were painfully aware of how much everyone hates 1-800 numbers because of the frustrating and time-consuming bouncing around that people are forced to endure.[†] What's the point of providing a 1-800 number to resolve a problem if the service itself is yet another problem? How do you make it a positive for the customer? We came up with this: answer the phone when it rings! Not with an automated voice but with a real live human being. How about saying hello? Then, asking "How can I help you?" and meaning it. Our customer service team had the authority to solve problems; they didn't have to put the customer on hold or steer them to another department or division. We wanted to get as far away as possible from the routine. We wanted

---

[*] The story is explored in detail in *The Orange Code*.

[†] Think toll-free numbers are relics from the past? True, they came into service back in 1966, but as *Forbes* reported recently, the numbers are still in very high demand and constitute "the primary phone line and support line since they add convenience to communicating with customers." In fact, there are now six additional prefixes besides the familiar 800. So why are customer service operations still so poor? (Vandita Jadeja and Rob Watts, "How to Get a Toll Free Number for Your Business," *Forbes*, November 1, 2023, forbes.com/advisor/business/get-a-toll-free-number/)

customers to know that we valued their time and that minimizing the time they spent on resolving a problem was an important goal.

I call this the "1-800 number problem": for millions of customers today, the frustrating lack of transparency is a major irritant and complaint. So why are we are still having problems? Consider the following: "Major banks, telecom giants, energy suppliers, and travel firms are burying their telephone numbers on obscure pages of their websites to deter customers from calling for help," a consumer news site reported recently.[1] In fact, "many companies are instead urging people to use 'live chat' services or demanding complaints be made via social media sites such as X." In one of the worst examples cited, customers were required to "click through six pages" on a major telecom's website "to find its phone number." Amazon has no number at all. A few companies surveyed went so far as to record online messages "advising customers not to bother ringing at all due to high wait times"; some were even forcing customers to "fill out an online form or answer a series of questions before revealing their helpline number."

> **Finding new customers is manifestly more complicated and expensive than keeping the ones you have.**

Remember, a 1-800 call is a direct form of customer feedback. So, what is being said about you and your brand if you are manufacturing complicated hurdles to prevent customers from reaching out? It is both shocking and a painful reminder of why leadership so often fails the culture test. One of the big lessons learned in Economics 101 is that finding new customers is manifestly more complicated and expensive than keeping the ones you have. Why take that kind of risk? The pool of potential customers is never as deep as one thinks. "We are new here" is a commitment to putting the customer experience first.

WHY CUSTOMER SATISFACTION IS SO IMPORTANT

The evidence is definitive. "The quality of customer experience offered by consumer-facing brands and government agencies declined in the year through April 2022," stated a study published by Forrester Research in June 2022.[2] Companies that scored a rating of "good" with customers declined 22 percent, "while the share of 'poor' and 'OK' scores increased." Another report noted that "challenges in customer relations are increasing as consumers complain more and say they obtain little satisfaction."[3] The trend is disturbing; even more so, however, are the implications for business.

According to a 2020 survey,[4] "some 66 percent of consumers surveyed in 2020 said they had experienced a problem with a product or service, up from 56 percent in 2017, when the survey was last conducted." And most of those, the survey noted, "said they weren't satisfied with the result. Indeed, 58 percent said they got nothing in return." Unfortunately, the end of the pandemic and our so-called return to normal hasn't much affected the dismal levels of consumer dissatisfaction. According to a 2023 report in the *Wall Street Journal*,[5] 74 percent of consumers surveyed said "they had experienced a product or service problem in the past year." In fact, the report noted, "Americans are encountering more problems with companies' products and services than ever before, and a higher proportion of them *are actively seeking 'revenge' for their troubles*" (my emphasis).

> **Start with the customer's needs and wants and work backward to create a system that satisfies you *and* them.**

The percentage of consumers who have taken action to settle a score against a company through measures such as pestering or public shaming in person or online tripled to 9 percent from 3 percent in 2020, according to the study. That reversed a downward trend with regards to revenge-seeking behaviour: the average percentage of customers seeking revenge between 2003 and 2017 was 17 percent.[6]

Are you still thinking that 1-800 number problem isn't a big deal?

• • •

No, not everyone jumped on board. We had customers who wanted the high savings rates, for instance, but demanded that ING Direct do things the same way as other banks. In fact, I fielded calls all the time from customers expecting exceptions. For them, we had a simple answer: We have one product and there are no exceptions. It's all we do. If you need more, please go to a bank with branches; they will be more than happy to accommodate you. They don't offer the same value or the same high interest rate on savings accounts, but that is what we do and what makes us new.

Many customers just didn't get it. Fine. We had customers who expected special treatment. "What should I do?" staff would ask. "Fire them," I said. We didn't want customers who were bad fits. Neither party benefitted. The culture we created worked. Customers in Canada (and not long after the United States) loved our direct approach and streamlined services. ING Direct became the first internet bank of scale and became the fifteenth largest bank in the United States. It all seems pretty obvious and straightforward now. But it always does. What I remember so clearly back then, however, was that nothing seemed certain. And that for me is what leadership turned out to be all about: transforming what is to what could be.

CULTURE IS ALL ABOUT CREATING POSITIVE MOMENTUM

A leader needs to not only communicate and to make understood the many aspects of the culture but repeat them again and again. Putting up motivational posters in the hallway or coffee room or sending out uplifting emails and newsletters are not enough. Culture needs to be lived and breathed every day. And it always starts with you as leader. *You are the culture.* As you go, so goes the culture. You are the cowboy in in the saddle. When the culture is alive, the horse knows where to go. The reins are just a reminder.

A COMMITMENT, NOT A SLOGAN

A commitment to "we are new here" is what kept ING Direct fresh and open to new ideas and opportunities. And that commitment applies wherever employees are on the company ladder. It's human nature to become comfortable with what works. But that can be what holds us back. An effective leader needs to know how to move the organization out of its comfort zone in order for everyone to flourish.

I remember I had been working for a large bank when I interviewed for a senior position with a major bank in Montreal. I was becoming well known as a "new ideas" kind of guy who knew how to shake things up and get it done. On paper, the new position seemed a perfect fit: they said they were looking for "new blood," which fit me to a tee. I was searching for a new challenge, someplace where I could make my mark by challenging the banking industry status quo. Having breezed through the first two interviews, I was given the impression that the final interview with the executive in charge of corporate banking was nothing more than a formality. The job was mine. I was really excited about getting started.

At that final interview, we talked as if we were colleagues about the history of the bank, the challenges it had experienced along the way, what I brought to the table, what they were hoping to accomplish, and about the many ways I could be an integral part of getting it done. I absolutely believed I had the job in the bag.

> Confidence is an important leadership feature; it's the mantra of the culture-driven leader.

Then, there were a few more questions: "Where did you grow up?" he asked. "Where do you consider home? *What kind of a name is Arkadi?*"

And just like that, the traffic light turned from green to red. I wasn't "the right fit." Years later, I found out he considered me "not one of us."

I was an immigrant kid who had arrived in Canada with nothing, so I was used to not fitting in. It bothered me, of course, being judged like that. It still does. What was the point, I thought on a number of occasions, banging my head against a door that will not open?

I didn't let it stop me, though, and years later, I had my chance to make a difference with ING Direct. It was a brand-new idea. No one in the banking industry — and I mean no one — took the idea seriously. "It isn't the way we do things."

"No," I thought. "It isn't. I'm new here."

RULES WERE MADE TO BE BROKEN

We hear that all the time, right? *Rules were made to be broken.* In many cases, that's true. It matters, however, which rules. Rules can be like the structure-bearing walls in a house; remove them and the house collapses. Culture-driven leadership requires a leader to know which rules need to be broken and which ones need to be retained and reinforced. Change that leads to enhanced customer experience, for instance, is to be encouraged; otherwise, change can undermine and weaken culture. In my experience, changes that were consistent with the culture (meaning, changes aligned with the principles) worked. It's like a river fed by many streams: the current needs to flow in one direction. It's important to remember that a culture is always in a defensive relationship with context. A culture can bend; it needs to be flexible enough to withstand buffeting forces. A culture that is too rigid will break; one that is too flexible will be overrun.

What appears permanent in a culture is not necessarily what needs over-throwing. For example, a leader can't juggle priorities; it can't be a focus on profits one day but on revenue the next. Culture has to have a familiar shape and form; it needs to be consistent. It has to be explained and easily understood. Do your customers understand your culture?* How about your employees? Most great artists rebel against an establishment and then be-come the establishment against which a new generation of artists rebel. A call to the barricades is dramatic, but not if no one shows up. A "we are new here" mindset displays an openness to fresh ideas and opportunities, but that doesn't mean that all new ideas are good ones. There's a need to prevent the kinds of (undesirable) change that will not benefit the culture. Change will

---

* Chances are very high, I suspect, that most of us would be confused about the overall state of our current politics, for instance. Increased divisiveness has created massive misalignments in what we consider normative behaviour. And the same might be true of the culture where you work. "Are we all on the same page?" Probably not. We might not even be reading the same book!

not be effective and will not improve anything if it's not clear why something needs changing and how. When change is enacted, reinforce it, make it the gold standard. When it needs to be revised, do it.

WHEN IN DOUBT, THERE IS NO DOUBT

Confidence is an important leadership feature; it's the mantra of the culture-driven leader. It entails projecting an air of certainty about the mission that is crucial. People who commit to you have to know you are in command.* The same holds for your customer. It's about trust.† Trust from your customer and your employees about who you are, where you're headed, and how you will get there. It's when a customer pays you the tribute of their continued loyalty, especially if it's unsolicited. A leader, after all, is in the service industry. You have to believe it. Your stakeholders have to believe it. Everyone on your team has to believe it. In other words, they all need certainty. They have to believe in you. That's where it starts, and that's where it ends.

THE X FACTOR

Leadership requires an X factor. It could be anything, but it's the thing that sets you as the leader apart. For me, the X factor was the chip on my shoulder.

As an immigrant growing up in Toronto, I was always being reminded that I didn't belong. Even when I learned how to fit in, I was still an outsider, which meant that every time I thought I had made it, thought about easing up, or resting on my laurels, I would hear that familiar nagging voice in my ear: *if you don't work harder and do more, if you don't conform, you'll never fit in.*

We are all immigrants, today especially. There is always something that sets us apart. It could be gender, it could be race, it could be politics or

---

* Hardly a day goes by without a news story about a CEO whose leadership is being openly and hostilely questioned by stakeholders, employees, and others. Social media, of course, has made it incredibly easy to attack leadership at a distance. The day-to-day challenge of projecting certainty has become formidable, and this, no doubt, has contributed to the increasingly short tenures for most business leaders.

† An easy mistake is confusing trust and certainty for arrogance. It is very hard to build trust; it requires time, effort, and consistency. Arrogance is a shortcut that more often than not undermines trust and certainty.

religion. At the same time, we have a lot more in common than what sets us apart. For instance, the reason that people trust business more than politics might be because business is more appealingly tribal than are traditional national identities (especially today when politics seems to have become highly confrontational). We all want to belong and feel valued and rewarded. We also want to believe we are doing something worthwhile.[*] "We are new here" means finding out what we have in common. It means looking over the fence, across the divide, outside the tribe. The Montreal executive who turned me down was a member of the C-suite that claimed it was a priority to find a candidate who could bring in a new perspective and some new blood. But why? Was it all for show? "We are new here" isn't just a slogan. It's the beating heart of the culture. It's what will bring your business to life and will sustain it throughout its life cycle.

NOT ONLY A STATE OF MIND

A few years after ING Direct in Canada was founded, our Dutch investors wanted to know if I was interested in heading up a new ING Direct venture in the United States. The idea of launching a revolution in banking in the biggest and highest-profile market in the world was an opportunity I could not say no to. It would also be a perfect opportunity to put to pasture circulating rumours in the top floors back in Amsterdam that the incredible success of ING Direct in Canada had been a very lucky shot in the dark.

I flew to Amsterdam to make my pitch. It went well, and before I knew it, I was flying back to Toronto with $250 million in capital commitment, no idea where I planned to open the U.S. offices, and a friendly reminder from our chairman that I had better not blow it. My colleague Jim Kelly and I embarked on a pilgrimage up and down the East Coast of the United States, but nothing felt quite right. We were running out of options. Driving down the I-95, Jim spotted a sign. *What about Wilmington?*

---

[*] "Employees increasingly value safe, healthy, stable and supportive work environments — especially those with strong leadership who are able to navigate through such hyper-uncertainty." (Kayla Webster, "8 Companies with the Highest Employee Retention," *Benefit News*, January 26, 2021, benefitnews.com/list/8-companies-with-the-highest-employee-retention)

"Where's that?"

"Delaware, I think."

It was not at all what we expected. What we found was a wonderful train station and a series of dilapidated industrial buildings standing along the Christina River. It was perfect! The rent was cheap, and the airport in Philadelphia was only a twenty-minute train ride away. I suggested we meet with the mayor. When he found out we were thinking about opening a new savings bank in a Second World War–era tannery building adjacent to the Christina River, he smiled, wished us good luck, and sent us on our way.

"What now?" Jim asked.

I noticed that the offices of U.S. senator Tom Carper were in the same building. "Let's see if he's in. Couldn't hurt, right?"

He was even more skeptical than the mayor. "Look, fellas," he said. "I love your enthusiasm. And I love your plans. Rehabilitating the riverfront is a number-one priority of mine." He paused. "You do know, however, that Delaware is the credit card capital of the world, right? Are you sure you wouldn't rather be selling credit cards?"

"Nope," I said. "I want to do something that's good for people." And what better way to be taken seriously than being the David that enters the ring against the giant Goliath. "We'll be new here. We'll show people there is a different way to do banking. Wilmington, Delaware, it is!"

He listened politely and wished us luck; over time, incidentally, he became a huge supporter of our new ideas, not only for the bank but the riverfront. (Energy and a desire to create and to feel a part of something new and exciting is infectious! Momentum!) Our Dutch investors were a bit cool to the idea at first too. I had promised to open a savings bank in the United States and instead was spending hundreds of thousands of dollars on an old tannery building in a city known as ground zero for credit cards. And the building wasn't even downtown with all the other big banking buildings.

"Arkadi, we're not sure you were the right choice. Maybe the United States venture is too much for you."

Talk about a hangs-in-the-balance leadership moment!

When in doubt, there is no doubt!

When in doubt, there is no doubt!

We persevered and pressed on. Not only did ING Direct become a financial success; our headquarters along the riverfront became a beloved landmark in Wilmington. Soon enough, other companies and entrepreneurs were buying up derelict buildings and warehouses along the riverfront and turning them into vital and vibrant spaces for everyone to enjoy. I was very proud to be an unofficial ambassador for Delaware!

It was a great example of the power of "we are new here" thinking. A leader must expect and anticipate resistance and understand how to live with doubt. It's in our nature to question behaviour that doesn't conform to convention. ING Direct was a revolutionary idea that no one believed could work ... until it did. But doubt cannot be part of your strategy. When my bosses had doubts, I could have agreed. "Yeah, on second thought, maybe you're right. I don't think I am up to this." But I was committed and knew I'd made a good choice. And I persuaded my bosses. I didn't succeed just thanks to charm or charisma, either. My partners and I had worked tirelessly on getting every detail, no matter how large or how small, *exactly right*. The thing is, as leader, you need to sell yourself *before* your leadership. In other words, who the messenger is matters. You need to be who they think you are. What that means is you finding out who they think you are!

Why? A leader needs to know how to get things done. It sounds simple, but it isn't at all. I'll be honest, I never had the slightest doubt that I could make ING Direct work. But so what? What I had to do was convince my bosses that I was the guy that could get it done. Leadership and goals had to line up perfectly. Had I approached a conventional bank with the same idea and pitched it in the same "we are new here" narrative, I would have been shown the door in seconds flat. A conventional bank would find (and did find!) such an idea inconceivable. The point: as a leader, you have to be believed.*

At the end of the day, did you get it done? It's how you'll be judged. It helps to have some luck, of course. Two ING Group executives, Hans

---

* A great example of a leader who wasn't believed was Disney's Bob Chapek. As we'll explore in a later chapter, Chapek was hand-picked in 2020 to succeed long-time Disney CEO Robert Iger, but his leadership style was wrong for the company, and he was canned. An able and experienced executive, Chapek's timing was awful.

Verkoren and Dick Harryvan, were on board and supported the project every step of the way. Hans in particular was one-of-a-kind and a very savvy leader; he had a well-tuned instinct for what would work with customers. Dick was the tactician who brought the discipline needed to every situation. Background-wise, we could not have been more different. Over time, however, we worked so well together we were known as the Three Musketeers. It was the complete opposite of my Montreal experience from years before. Here I was, an immigrant, a Canadian spearheading an American venture on behalf of Dutch investors. We had nothing in common — except a shared vision and a willingness to do it different, do it better. We had a cause. None of that other stuff mattered. It was the power of "we are new here" dynamics.

WHAT'S YOUR CAUSE?

I was sitting having coffee in the conference room with Jim Kelly. At that point, ING Direct was five years into its existence, growing by $1 billion in deposits a month. It was surreal. It had all started so simply: just a blank sheet of paper and a dream. There hadn't been many rules then, just belief and inclination. Since then, however, the scale of the operations had grown beyond belief, and the levels of complexity had exploded exponentially. We had this enormous beast on our hands. Jim and I talked about the challenges ahead, and the inevitable question came up: Is this what we want to be do doing for the next five or ten years? Are we the right team to carry on? Can rebels who wanted to upend an industry be happy as the establishment?

Every business is a three-act play: birth, maturity, death.* Can one move from Act I (the startup) and cross over to managing a mature business that has grown in Act II? And what happens after that? Were we prepared? Businesses grow, of course, but does leadership grow along with it? Or are different skills and leadership styles required? Jim and I had seen that every year one or more of the original leadership team had left. There are reasons why teams break up, of course, personal or professional; keeping a winning

* The three stages of business will be discussed in more detail in chapter 2.

team together is very hard. Knowing when to quit and turn over leadership to someone else is a very difficult call. If events push you out, it's too late. If you quit too early, you will be haunted by the "what ifs."

We finished our coffee that morning and agreed that we would reframe the narrative. Let's not focus on dry details like growth, size and scale, quotas, we decided. Instead, let's radically adjust our perspective. Let's pretend we are starting fresh every day. Just like we did with the startup. That's when we came up with "we are new here today." It seemed perfect; after all, hadn't that been what we had been doing all this time?

In our case, however, the slogan wasn't simply a way of describing a strategy; the slogan was the culture. Every day we would come into work and look at what we were doing — how we were doing it — with fresh eyes. What could we do better? And we expected the same from our employees and customers. "Do you see us as new?" we wanted to know. "Are we getting it right?" "Are we worth your loyalty?" If not, we weren't doing our jobs. If we weren't solving problems, we were the problem. Complacency that results in a loss of focus on the customer experience is the most dangerous threat to a business in its mature phase.

If we weren't solving problems, we _were_ the problem.

Even in the startup mode, a reset and rethink should be welcomed. Early change, if necessary, is the difference between success or failure. Zenbanx needed a reset a number of times. It was the steady hand of Tom Hugh in finance that was critical to making it work. Unruffled, Tom always met the challenge head on and worked for the right answers. Leadership by example. It takes a team of different skills and independent views to make execution of the business plan a success.

We are all in this together. It doesn't matter whether you joined the team at the very start or yesterday. Every day, we all walk up to the same starting line. How can we all work together to reach our goal today? How can we do it better? How can we enhance customer experience?

BETTER, NOT BEST

We've all heard of Occam's razor: it's the principle that it's better to opt for the simpler answer or explanation over the more complicated. The same is true for "we are new here."* Not every idea has to be a million-dollar winner. What's important is being open to rethinking and revising operations in ways that may not be remarkable but that actually make a difference. When the focus is on improving customer experience, it all adds up.

For example, in 2012 I helped found a company that would allow customers to create a foreign-currency chequing account that would allow them to hold multiple currencies and pay in those currencies without having to exchange funds on every transaction. That way, customers could skip the usual per-transaction fees. Zenbanx would be great for mobile customers who work, live, or have assets in more than one country, we thought. In the early days, we had hundreds of conversations about what did not work and how it would have to work. Getting back to basics; doing what hasn't been done. Keeping it simple and making it easy to understand, to access and to use. That is the Zenbanx culture. *Around the block; around the world.*

> It's not always about reinventing the wheel; it can be about making that wheel even rounder.

Planning another startup, I recall we openly discussed ideas, strategy, products, and services that could work and be created to disintermediate other products that did not work well. We spent a lot of time and effort trying to build *the best* product we could. In my experience, leaders often focus too much on replacing what exists in the marketplace instead of focusing on building a good product and pushing ahead with a simpler but better solution — *the rounder wheel.* It was true in my case. I wanted best when good would have been better. We were in Silicon Valley at the time, however, where nothing seems impossible and nothing but the best will

---

* We'll be exploring this idea in more depth in chapter 4.

do. Let's reach for the stars! Let's build the best product ever! It sounded great. But ...

I should have listened to my instincts and heeded my concerns that we were pushing too hard. We eventually ran out of capital. It was a big lesson for me about what it means to innovate *meaningfully*. "Build a better solution and they will come" is true, but the process is not without limitations. *Better*, sometimes, *not always best*. The capital and resources required to match adoption and growth outcomes must, in turn, lead to profit in order to survive. I knew it but was too wrapped up in the Silicon Valley mindset.

Holding close to your own counsel — trusting it — is never easy. As I have experienced many times, being able to keep your feet on the ground and your head "above the clouds" — finding the right balance when in the whirlwind of creating a new product or service — is tricky.

"When there is doubt ..."

Remember, a leader's primary responsibility is to create and instill confidence and to eliminate doubt. "When there is doubt there is no doubt" is a leadership mantra made popular by the U.S. Marine Corps. Follow your instincts; they are more often right than not. Everyone needs to believe that the path is right and that the mission is going to succeed. To believe and commit means believing in the leader who convinced you, that it will be a good and successful outcome.

At the opening of this chapter, I said that "we are new here" is an across-the-board commitment to positive customer experience, and that commitment has to be believed and embraced at every level of the company or business. It has to be lived on a daily basis. It's about thinking past the initial purchase stage, for instance, to the *What happens next?* stage. That is what customer experience *means*. It's an experience — the total sum of events — not a single event. I'm happy with my purchase today, but what about tomorrow? Next week? A month or year from now? "We are new here" can't be a slogan or a gimmick plastered on promotional material. A leader needs to be reviewing company culture and asking of it, "How is this serving the best interests of our customer?" And then making sure it does. Think of all the products and services we use, and we can see endless opportunities to improve, to make new and better all around. Our world is being inundated by new products and services, and all of it is being delivered at a massive scale that has consequences (most of them unforeseen) for society, culture, the climate, and Mother Earth. Can we do better?

Not too long ago, I was drawn in as a consultant for a new banking venture in Silicon Valley (where I live). As one would expect, the team I met was young, confident, brashly enthusiastic, and absolutely determined to "break models" and "push boundaries." Their pitch was sharp, high energy, state of the art. Applause, applause. I was asked what I thought, and it was only as I waded into the dry and dull details of the fantastically complex federal and regulatory hurdles they would have to address that I felt the momentum stall. I could feel the energy level drop. I had become what is known as the "buzz kill." They just did not want to hear about it. *Dude, what is your problem? We have this great idea. It's a killer. Totally revolutionary.*

> **Commitment has to be believed and embraced at every level of the company or business.**

On the ride home from that meeting, I realized what the problem was: "These guys have no clue what they're up against. They have something new, but they don't know anything about what it means to *be new*. It's like everyone in the Valley has a magic wand." What I hadn't heard was anyone talking about who their customers were or who they wanted them to be, what customers said they needed as opposed to what the startup team was convinced they needed, and how they intended to deliver a better customer experience. Thinking outside the box is important; just don't forget why the box exists in the first place. It could be the new (better) approach is building a better box. Innovation and novelty are wonderful. Technology, for instance, has revolutionized business around the world. And continues to do so. But "we are new here" leadership is focused on more than just technology or innovation. It's about innovation directed at enhanced and improved customer experience. Effective leadership is knowing which is which.

CONCLUDING THOUGHT

Leaders will be at the forefront of the effort to build a culture that can serve not only all stakeholders but answer a higher calling. In other words, *Is this the right thing to be doing? Can we be doing it better? Who benefits? Who is being left behind and what can we do about that?* We need to think ahead of time about what we do and how we are dealing with all these *unforeseen* consequences. Time is critical, and how we lead and how we perform makes a difference; the bar has been set and each day it is set higher.

"We are new here." That is the enduring call for a leader.

ACTION POINTS

- An effective leader who embodies the "we are new here" ethos will be an inspiration for others to do the same.
- There is no escape from context; think of human nature, in fact, as the most conspicuous form of context. It cannot be controlled.
- Find a cause that can help unite people around a common goal or outcome. It needs to be shared, understood, and valued.
- Did you get it done? It's how you'll be judged.
- Principle-based culture needs buy-in from the top to the bottom, no exceptions.
- Face every day with fresh eyes and a willingness to meet the challenges ahead in new and meaningful ways. Working every day with a new sense of tomorrow drives growth and opportunity.
- When in doubt there is no doubt: you — the leader — have to be believed.

Chapter 2

WE ARE HERE TO CREATE, NOT DESTROY

It doesn't matter what business you are in, how big or small: creating and building is the common thread of work. Creating means improving, replacing the outdated with the updated, always revising and refreshing, focusing on better, innovating, yes, but with an eye always on preserving what works and respecting and valuing the "broader" mission that is crucial to the culture. It's remembering that growth is fine, but "too big" is a threat to the culture. It's a positive approach and outlook. It's often misunderstood.

How?

• • •

The most difficult task a leader faces today is focusing on the basics.

Consider the following example. In 2020 Peloton, the sensationally popular at-home fitness company, was (pardon the pun) riding high, and co-founder and CEO John Foley could do no wrong. *And then he did.* Stock prices, which had reached a high of $170 per share, dropped 80 percent in just two years to a low of $29. Foley found himself operating unawares in a suddenly and radically altered context. It began in late 2019 when Peloton released a Christmas holiday advertisement featuring a husband gifting his young wife one of its trademark stationary bikes. At the time the ad aired, the company's stock was soaring. The social media backlash to the ad, however, was immediate and scorching. It was denounced and mocked as sexist and (given the product's hefty price tag) "classist," even "dystopian."

In December 2021, company shares fell to their lowest level in nineteen months after a favourite character on the wildly popular series *Sex and the City* suffered a fatal heart attack after working out on a Peloton. "There's no such thing as bad publicity," said P.T. Barnum. He never had to deal with social media. Fans were so shocked and upset that investors took note: "a link" — even a completely fictional link — between "the company's eponymous exercise bike and the possibility of a heart attack"[1] was enough to create a downward stampede.

Culture-driven leaders must always be aware and awake to threats and challenges to the brand.

Foley — perhaps channelling his inner Caesar — was dismissive of the social media backlash, considering it no real threat to the company's elevated position in the marketplace. "We don't have to do much more in order to have one of the greatest consumer companies of the next couple of decades," he told reporters at an investor conference. "Fitness equipment has been a dopey category with dopey products." The industry was an "albatross we are trying to shake as we build one of the most innovative companies of our day."

Foley shrugged off any concern for customers or any backlash. "If you're thinking hard about getting a treadmill, I don't know where you're going to go." Foley even suggested that using the Peloton device "may have even helped delay" the TV character's "cardiac event."[2]

Instead of limiting the backlash, Foley's crisis-management missteps only added momentum to the cascade of bad news. When the company cut its digital subscription price, investors worried it meant the company "was prioritizing growth over profitability," and downward momentum pushed stock prices ever lower. Even two years later, Foley seemed disconnected from reality. "The stock going backwards is a bit of a head-scratcher, I've got to be honest with you," Foley conceded.

One expert who analyzed the situation suggested that a significant portion of the company's valuation was based on "the very long customer relationships that the market" expected Peloton "to have with its customers." In other words, the stock price was tied very directly to *customer satisfaction.*

One raindrop does not, of course, foretell a storm, but several raindrops should at least give one pause. By February 2022, charges of "mismanagement of the company" by its CEO and demand for change forced Foley to step down "after an extended streak of tumult," which, by the way, also resulted in the company cutting three thousand jobs.†

Emotional intelligence is a very important leadership metric. Leadership demands self-awareness,‡ empathy, social awareness, and conflict management skills. To ensure that they "create rather than destroy," culture-driven leaders must always be aware and awake to threats and challenges to the brand. *What are they? Where are they coming from?* and *What needs to done?* Performance metrics like novelty, market dominance, or profits are not necessarily reliable predictors or indicators. Leadership that assumes one can successfully ignore or downplay customer preferences or priorities (in other words, changes of context) is dangerously blinkered.

A company like Peloton was the "it girl" of the moment. What that means in practical terms is that the difference between what's new and what's not is a simple function of time. What happened to John Foley, to a talented executive, occurs more often than we might think. What worked at an early stage of Peloton's trajectory suddenly stopped working. An effective leader needs to see the dark clouds on the horizon and have a plan.

---

* As we keep repeating, it's not what you think customers want or what you decide will satisfy a customer; it's always what the customer thinks. According to the simple metric of "customer satisfaction," it shouldn't be difficult to identify where and how leaders go wrong.

† Anyone interested in a deep-dive exploration into a textbook example of how easy it is to lose focus should consider the incredible fall from grace of the BlackBerry from Research In Motion.

‡ Speaking of awareness, back when Peloton had actually granted permission to the TV show to product-place their popular exercise machine, no one at Peloton had bothered to find out "the context of the appearance." *No such thing as bad publicity?*

Time can (and most likely will) kill any brand. Poor leadership or a radical change in context (or more often a combination of both) can result in premature brand irrelevance. A goal of culture-driven leadership is to maximize brand relevance as experienced by the customer. It's about focusing on the basics.

EAT OR BE EATEN? A TOUGH CALL

Humans are tool-making animals. It is fundamental to our nature to invent and create. To take what we see and see farther. Innovation arrives so quickly and in so many varieties and versions that what is new is obsolete upon arrival. The difference between old and new, in other words, is only a function of time. And as leaders, we have less and less time to find a path away from obsolescence. Are we here to create or destroy? Increasingly, the answer is ... both.

A strong business culture will focus on inventing new ways of performing and of creating new products. Truth is, no business can escape its "sell before" date. Obsolescence will catch up with every business; leaders today need to deal with that simple fact, and they need to recognize the probability that obsolescence is much closer than one might think. Products and services do not last; they wear out or lose favour with customers, are replaced by better ones. Sometimes, markets simply disappear. None of this is new.

Along with all the great things that it can engender, innovation also can be a catalyst to unexpected and unforeseeable negative consequences and disruptions. Not that long ago, entertainment companies like Tower Records and Blockbuster enjoyed market dominance, but both disappeared without a trace. And what about the Sony Walkman? It's easy in retrospect to plot the course of market disruption, decline, and demise, and offer informed eulogies on what *should have been done*. Leaders, however, never have the predictive luxury of the "backward glance." Judgments and decisions about the future direction of the market and one's place in it have to be made in the present. The key is judging the timeline and speed of change. For the leader, this is hard-choices time. Why?

A complacent culture will adopt a "wait it out" or "let's wait and see" approach. *We're fine. Relax.* The culture-driven leader, on the other hand, will be awake to context and act pre-emptively (if possible). A culture that is proactive will revise and refresh its own products and services before unhappy customers and competitors do it. In other words, *Let's do this. Then we'll be fine.*

The discipline required to make these kinds of forward-focused judgments is difficult, and *extremely* difficult to sustain over time: doing now, in the short term, what will create benefits in the long term requires courage. For one thing, you will open yourself up to doubt, dissent, and escalating levels of second-guessing. Not everyone will buy in immediately. There might be real casualties. Again, though, the leader needs always to be thinking long-term when making decisions. A culture that says, "Okay, today is a new day and we can do better than yesterday," and has the courage and willingness to incur the costs and effort required to continually create for tomorrow is very difficult to create and foster. A company whose culture is built to "read" context and can accommodate the "bigger picture" — i.e., the larger value and the power of the business that align when an enterprise is competitively positioned on the leading edge — has better odds of sustaining winning results.

> **No business can escape its "sell before" date. Obsolescence will catch up with every business.**

Getting it right is the true test.

TIMING

A leader cannot judge or manage the creation of products and services alone. It takes everyone. Getting the timing and creation of new products and services right is the most difficult thing to achieve. The project manager plays the central role today in growing a business. If "creating rather than destroying" is a value shared by everyone, setbacks and failures incurred "getting it right" become manageable, as does the ability to *collectively* recover and move forward. The ability to accept failure and learn from it and move forward is a valuable but difficult cultural value to trust. SpaceX is a good example of having this quality. It risked bankruptcy but it prevailed and won the race to get Americans back into space.

Remember: if you're wrong, it's all on you. It never matters what you *tried to do* or what you had *hoped to do*. No one cares. Next is a perfect example of the right-leader wrong-context problem.

THE DAVID SOLOMON AND GOLDMAN SACHS QUESTION

In late January 2023, the financial giant Goldman Sachs issued its quarterly earnings report. The financial sector was not amused. Losses totalled almost $3 billion, and — immediately — blame was directed at CEO David Solomon. Having taken over leadership of the company in 2018 promising "major restructuring," he was now being criticized for causing "major upheaval inside the bank."* Efforts by Solomon "to streamline the bank's culture and practices, and to better orient the firm toward a future in which technology is likely to sap the ability of big banks to make money as intermediaries," had the effect of alienating executives "who were frustrated with Mr. Solomon's leadership style."[3] The restructuring included merging "fragmentary fiefs" in one division and doing away with "antiquated rivalries between different groups of bankers." Solomon had assured the board that the changes "were Goldman's only way forward in an era when technology threatens to weaken the traditional financial system's hegemony," and they had agreed.

Solomon's leadership style and decisions, however, drew "widespread criticism from investors and analysts," as well as from a dozen senior executives who were fed up and decided to head for the exit. His abrasive and dismissive leadership style, it was alleged, had "created enough friction among senior employees that it could undermine the success of his strategy."

---

* Entities like boards of directors can be notoriously fickle and inconsistent. Solomon — like Disney's former CEO Bob Chapek — had earned unanimous support from his board. "We're with you … until we aren't." Never count on your support, in other words.

Solomon, it was reported, "rules with an iron fist." Whereas his predecessor had a more collegial and congenial leadership style where input was encouraged, his critics contended Solomon "spurns dissent, appears unwilling to entertain criticism and has been known to yell at meetings" — a style "that has fallen especially out of favor after the coronavirus pandemic upended traditional notions of work and work-life balance."[*]

Solomon has his defenders, too. A Goldman Sachs spokesperson stated, "His style is 'direct,' but he's running a big, complex business." Pointing out that "it was not unusual to have different views about a chief executive's style," he insisted Solomon "had shown flexibility." For instance, he said, "If a strategy isn't meeting our aspirations, David has shown the ability to adjust and pivot."

A banking analyst questioned by the *New York Times* about the announcement and Solomon's style commented: "He has a mission, and that mission is not to be the most-liked person at the firm."

Who's right? Was Solomon *the right executive* at the right time? Was he swinging a big stick in a "we need this now" effort to disrupt what had become a comfortable and complacent executive elite? Had he read the culture correctly — identified where the structural problems were — and struck proactively? *Better wrack up losses now than wait until it's too late and see huge losses later.* Or was it the opposite? Did he get the culture completely wrong? Was it all about disruption for its own sake? I don't know, of course, but neither does anyone else. Only time will tell. And that is something that fewer and fewer leaders have. Solomon might have found himself on the short plank, but it is just as likely his leadership will turn out to be just what the doctor ordered, and he will be hailed as a genius. What's a fact is that David Solomon is being paid a huge salary to get it right. Whether he gets enough time and support to see it through is a question.[†]

---

[*] By the way, the comment is a beautiful example of how hard (but necessary) it is for any leader to correctly "read" and adapt to changes in context. In this case, the "traditional notions of work and work-life balance" represent a potentially massive misalignment between leadership style and culture.

[†] As we know, the same is true for Disney's current CEO Robert Iger as well as former CEO Bob Chapek. Was Chapek the right leader with the right ideas but operating inside the wrong context? Will Iger's leadership (the corporate embodiment of Disney culture) succeed where his predecessor failed? Culture over context?

CHAOS IS EASY; DISRUPTION IS HARD

It's hard to disrupt a marketplace. As customers, we become accustomed to how we navigate products and services. If a new way appears, it isn't an automatic that it will be adopted. It has to be accepted, for one thing, as better. But better than what? The culture-driven leader must always keep in mind that it doesn't matter if it's better according to your interpretation; it has to be considered better by the customers. For that to happen, the benefits need to be easily seen and understood. Success is measured on adoption and growth. Finding the right formula is not easy and timing is everything. Too early and the education of the marketplace is expensive. Too late, then the field is crowded and it's expensive to compete for customers. Finding the right timing and demonstrating value and getting customers to pay the new price or value of a product or service is hard to do.

If disruption is not followed by *adoption* and *growth*, that's chaos. Disruption is not only about *challenging* behaviour but revising it so as to align with the culture. It answers the "What now?" question with "Here's how." Why is this important? For me, the most exciting and energizing aspects of being a CEO are taking on the marketplace, facing the competition, and risking a plan that customers will validate or reject. It's the hunt. Finding a way to evolve behaviour is not easy! Just look at the news; no one agrees with anyone anymore. It's also not linear. It only looks easy in hindsight. But for a leader, that's the challenge: transforming an organization where very little alignment existed into one whose culture is embraced by all. If you can do that, you know you have built something really special.

> The most exciting and energizing aspects of being a CEO are taking on the marketplace, the competition, and risking a plan that customers will validate or reject.

Whenever a startup or new business is launched, there are always people who say it won't succeed. Throughout my life as a CEO, there have always been people who have told me that the risks are too high, it can't work, I should play it safe. Remember, you're the one at the front of the line. What you hear is coming from everyone standing behind you. They don't know what you see. You job as leader is to make them see what you see. For me, it always helped to remind myself that I am by nature an outsider, a rebel. What choice did I really have? Nothing will happen unless someone wants it to happen, right? Who will that someone be?

No matter where you find yourself on the leadership ladder, remember that learning how to be a great CEO is no different from mastering any other skill. You learn and you experience and you refine your knowledge and abilities in order to execute well. Experience counts, of course, but you always need to be self-aware and learning and adapting. Today I can handle people and work in a more effective way than ever before. I've seen it all, I think, until the new situation is standing right in front of me. As leader, you're reinventing the wheel over and over.

SUCCESS HAS MANY MOTHERS AND FATHERS, BUT FAILURE IS AN ORPHAN

Leadership is not for the faint of heart. You take the hit when it goes wrong. There are regrets and post-mortems, of course. You cannot always be right. You make mistakes. What you may not be fully aware of on the front side of you career is how many personal sacrifices you will be forced to make. The time and attention the job required that kept you from family or friends, for instance. The weekends you spent stuck in the office. It's just what you have to do. Your job as leader precludes regrets. You have to be right a lot more than you are wrong, which is an enormously heavy burden to lug around all the time. It means decisions can't be made lightly or on the spur of the moment. If you're lucky, the people around will understand; chances are, however, they won't. It's not easy to admit it, but that's a fact of leadership life. You never have a day off. The pressures and the stress are unbelievable, and if you have never experienced it, it's worth your time to think seriously about whether you are the right person for the journey. Not everyone is. Most of us can leave our job at work. A leader is never not working. You have to be pretty good to stay in the role, and you have to win. It's the nature of any business and leadership role. That is never going to change.

On the other hand, success needs to be shared, because that's where it comes from. You can't do it alone. I remember very well ING Direct team members promoting "our" successes; and that was fine. *It is always a team win.* Your job as the culture-driven leader is to own the loss but share the win. If losses or mistakes need to be acknowledged, do it directly, transparently, and immediately. Get it back on track as soon as possible. The key piece of the leadership triage is to make sure you are clear to *everyone* about the mission. Keep all eyes to the bigger picture! Fingers start pointing when factions emerge, or rival incentives are allowed to develop. Sharing a mission that includes an "above the clouds" perspective helps break down tribal rivalries and promotes investment in shared outcomes.

> Success needs to be shared. You can't do it alone.

BUILDING LEADERSHIP CAPITAL

A leader needs a track record. Why would I follow you? Even a leader like Ulysses S. Grant needed to prove himself before he consolidated his position as commander of the Union forces. And the humility and generosity with which he treated his enemy was a lasting tribute of his leadership. But it came at a huge cost. There was never a moment in his early days as leader where the outcome was not in doubt. Success is never destined.[*]

The right to challenge the market (or to build another company) is only granted based on your last successful campaign. "What have you done lately?" If you succeed, smart money reasons you're the safe bet to repeat.

---

[*] In his *Memoirs*, American Civil War general and president Ulysses S. Grant described an early childhood superstition that revealed a lot about his potential as a leader: "When I started to go anywhere, or to do anything, [I made it a point] not to turn back until the thing intended was accomplished." Biographer Josiah Bunting adds that as a boy Grant "was game; he was curious" and "predisposed" by an early fatalism "to make the best of things." Grant "was a watcher, slow in passing judgment, comfortable in going his own way ... full of the quiet self-reliance that made him act rather than explain himself." To others, however, "It was widely accepted that he would fail." The qualities that make for great leadership, in other words, are often not immediately visible — to others, of course, but even to ourselves.

Investors like upside and try to minimize risk. This is the "thinking pool" a leader swims in. In today's world, the pressure to succeed is very strong. There's a lot of pressure, with everything on the line. A leader can't escape the "all-in with everything on the line." You have to show commitment, conviction, and passion. *It is all personal.* Production and deployment timelines have shrunk and the margin for error has disappeared. Even for a leader of a small company, of ten or so, for instance, finding and creating alignment about goals, missions, strategies, and outcomes can be difficult. Think about a hundred employees, or a thousand. Where do you find the alignments? How do you keep them aligned?

"WE'RE WITH YOU ... UNTIL WE AREN'T"

Alignment is a huge issue for leaders.

Consider a rather obvious fact about business: the number of products and services that have failed dwarfs the number that have succeeded. Success is hard. We celebrate the winners and forget the failures. Life moves on. Success has many mothers and fathers, right? But failure is an orphan. A leader understands it. Accepts it. A culture that values creating and understands and appreciates it as a natural process on an evolutionary path from inception to dissolution is exceptional.

The more context-focused we are, the more short-term our focus is. In this case, the temptation is to abandon or rethink the game plan. And that might be necessary. It's halftime, for instance, and your team is down by thirty-five points. The fans are stunned. *Oh my god, what's happening?* Panic and confusion set in, and immediately a hunt begins for someone to blame. It happens everywhere, in businesses large and small. Even the healthiest culture is not immune. It's a reality every business and every CEO will experience. Chances are, the experienced coach will use halftime to remind the players to be patient, that it isn't over, that they need to focus on the basics and not try to do too much too soon. Even in the chaos of the short term, be thinking long term.

The culture-driven leader's job is to get people to keep their focus on culture, not context. This keeps people aligned. We all want alignment. It makes the process run smoothly and efficiently. The reality is that alignment is very hard to achieve and difficult to maintain. Context is always threatening alignment. No two people are ever going to agree completely. The zones of alignment tend to become smaller and smaller as more voices are added to the mix. For a leader, the obligation is not necessarily to achieve the Holy Grail of perfect alignment; rather, it's finding and cultivating the alignments that work and managing the ones that don't.

I have been in meetings with investors in various startups who were jumping out of their shoes to "buy in." They couldn't have been more enthusiastic about what I was proposing or how it would work and what the value would be. All the things that I valued — everything we are reading about in this book! — they met with thumbs-up enthusiasm. "Fantastic!" "We love it." "What do you need?" It usually doesn't take long to discover, however, that buy-in comes condition- or time-stamped: shared *values* are not the same as shared *interests*. Shared interests, in other words, are not always shared. The "above the clouds" approach, ironically, means getting underneath the apparent alignment to find out what is really going on. Possible sources of misalignments can be identified by assessing who is on board versus who is on board up to "this" or "that" point. It could make all the difference in the world to your tenure as leader to know which is which.

Circumstance (context) drives a lot of these dynamics.

"YOUR UNCLE BOB IS HERE ..."

Here's a classic example of how alignment (and misalignment) can be imagined. It's a classic moment: you've assembled the perfect team, everyone has been working their rear ends off for months, you're on track. It all looks great ... until Uncle Bob shows up. And just like that, all that positive momentum is derailed.

I had a routine with people I hired. I asked them to think of a happy family occasion. Okay, once they had that in their mind, I asked them to now think of an unhappy family occasion. "Don't tell me what happened," I said. "Your Uncle Bob showed up." It was amazing how often I was right.

Every organization — every team, no matter how large or small — has an Uncle Bob. Disruption is what he does; he can't help it. We all have an Uncle Bob. Whatever precautions you take or whatever you try to do, it doesn't matter. An Uncle Bob will show up. It's important for a leader to keep in mind that anyone can be an Uncle Bob under the right (or wrong) circumstances. The disruptive Uncle Bob on your team needs to be identified and (if necessary) sidelined. If the disruption is of a magnitude or scale that smooth operations are jeopardized, he needs to be fired. Just remember that a member of your team who is fired is a reflection on you and your leadership.

Obviously, hiring well is key. But even if a great team has been assembled, there's no guarantee of alignment. The challenge is *sustaining the right team* over time. Think of the team as a huge jigsaw puzzle where the pieces keep changing. People are not robots, right? And every once in a while, an Uncle Bob shows up. It's why buying into the culture and making sure everyone continues to be invested is so important: high, enthusiastic, and sustained cultural buy-in is a good way of red-lighting the appearance of Uncle Bobs.

BUSINESS IS A THREE-ACT PLAY

Business as a three-act play. It helps to remember this when thinking about creating rather than destroying. So how does it work? In Act I, we have a startup. The mature stage is Act II and, it follows, the demise is Act III. This seems obvious. What isn't obvious is that each act requires a different kind of leadership, a different kind of perspective, different skills, and different priorities. But the culture is the same.

Early on in the building phase of ING Direct (Act I), for instance, it became clear our financial backers were interested in a conventional, profit-driven banking model, while my management team and I were focused on building a "new" kind of deposit savings bank with an emphasis squarely on savings. We were after the customers who had become disillusioned by traditional banks. The two objectives were not necessarily mutually exclusive; presumably, both goals could be met. The new bank would need both:

new approaches to make a profit and a business plan that would deliver lower costs and better margins.

What went wrong?

There was a debate about which products should be built and launched first: assets (loans) or liabilities (deposits). The next debate was about the scale and amounts. What was needed more, early profits or early volumes? Both carried risk and the resulting budgeting process became very difficult to balance. Neither objective was wrong; the problem was setting priorities: Which takes the lead? As long as we were making progress, there was give and take. If things slowed down, when we hit a pothole in the road, we found ourselves in increasingly acrimonious debates about trust and confidence. On one side, the staff, the customers, and the market overall all seemed to believe in the brand and the mission. The U.S. media market (the culture) overwhelmingly applauded a savings bank with an empathetic approach to everyday customer concerns. Word of mouth built the reputation and the deposits stuck and did not churn. The savings rate was higher than the market average (a cost that to a bean-counting profit-only-perspective could have been lower). At what price? would the other side ask. And with what end result? What was more important, the bigger profit or the bigger franchise?

Not all sectors, of course, were anxious to promote increased saving, but we had our evangelists, and we were signing up more and more each month, so we figured we must have been doing something right. Yes, it would take time. New and great ideas all need time to develop roots. Luckily, the shareholders were patient and had deep pockets. The customers did not always push for the highest rate, and loyalty rates based on excellent service were high. Defection rates were very low. Even so, the tension and misalignment that began on day one lasted for twelve years.

It was a fact of ING Direct life in Act I and through Act II, and as a leader, I had to learn how to manage to the satisfaction of both parties. Act III arrived in the form of the financial crisis of 2007–2008. The final sale of the bank ended well, and the valuation rewarded the shareholders eventually. Unfortunately, it ended the goal of the employees and management to keep building the franchise and the mission to lead Americans back to savings.

Could it have ended differently? Could the bank have just continued with different shareholders? Possibly, yes. However, potential suitors with the wherewithal made it clear they wanted cheaper deposits and did not share our valuation of the ING Direct brand as good for customers. In other words, they got the *financials*; what they couldn't (or wouldn't) appreciate was the *culture*, the value of the brand and its reputation with the customer base. Meanwhile, investors who highly valued the franchise and brand could not raise the capital. The profit margins were just too small compared to conventional banks.

Remember that perfect alignment is not possible; instead, find the alignments that are both necessary and beneficial to the mission; minimize the distraction of those that aren't.

In 2017 I experienced once again how misalignment can doom a company. When the owners of Zenbanx sold our tech startup to the online lending company SoFi, there was a lot of disappointment among the 120 employees. Some were disappointed in the outcome, of course; others just shrugged and moved on. Most, however, wanted assurances that it was a job that had been worth having. That it had been the right cause and a worthwhile experience … not just for employees but for the customers. It was! And I wanted them to know it.

When I talked with them, I remember quite a few specifically mentioning that in explaining to potential customers the Zenbanx story, what it was attempting to do, how it was a new financial product that was upending conventional banking practices, it excited them and convinced them not only that new opportunities were constantly on the horizon but that they could be involved. Testimony like that was incredibly gratifying.

I was especially pleased that SoFi CEO Mike Cagney seemed to understand what we were all about and shared our values.* "The true way to think about market opportunity here is around lifetime value of the customer, not around transactional economics," he told a financial magazine at the time

---

* Temporarily, at least. In October 2023 SoFi offered $250 cash back for new accounts. The small print: to earn the full bonus, "customers must open a SoFi Checking and Savings account and have direct deposits of $5,000 or more within 25 days." New kid on the block? Or just "business as usual"? (Ariana Arghandewal, "SoFi Checking and Saving account review 2024," CNN Underscored, November 15, 2023, cnn.com/cnn-underscored/reviews/sofi-checking-savings-review)

of the sale.[4] A company news release elaborated: "SoFi and Zenbanx share a vision that banking can and should be a lot better, and that's what's at the heart of this deal. Zenbanx founder and CEO Arkadi Kuhlmann was on the front lines of the branchless banking revolution in the late 1990s as the founder of both ING Direct USA and ING Direct Canada. Under his leadership, ING Direct USA became the largest direct bank in the country, largely because they could do things over the phone and online that incumbent banks couldn't."

Unfortunately, it turned out to be a very brief honeymoon. Less than eight months after the acquisition, SoFi switched priorities and shut us down. It was a very fast third act. And that is another hard lesson a leader has to learn. You can only do so much. Seldom can a leader balance and align all the variables; if it can be done, it's very hard to keep it together for a long time.[*]

. . . .

You never know when opportunity is going to knock or what it will look like. *Always be ready.*

. . . .

In an amazing story about reversals of fortune and the hard-to-kill shelf life of good ideas, in late 2023 we were approached by a new group of investors keen to finance a promising venture. It turned out Zenbanx — the company SoFi already had but did not support — was exactly what they were looking for. I became founder and CEO of a fresh and invigorated iteration of Zenbanx. Did I ever lose faith in the product? No. Had I been disappointed? *Absolutely.* Leaders don't often get second kicks at the can. In my case, I am back in the industry where I made my mark with a product I believe in and one I believe customers will believe in too. And, hopefully, I am still stirring it up a bit! Point is, you never know when opportunity is going to knock or what it will look like. *Always be ready.*

---

[*] If it helps, imagine your business as a small spinning planet where everything is always under centrifugal (outward directed) pressure to fly off into space. Your job as leader is to create centripetal (centre directed) pressure as a counteraction.

CONTEXT CHANGES LEADERSHIP

Context changes leadership and how leadership is defined. It was not so long ago that Christopher Columbus was revered as a hero and a courageous explorer; today he is reviled as a brutal imperialist who committed genocide, destroying the native population of the places he explored. Talk about a context change. In Britain's moment of crisis in the Second World War, Winston Churchill rallied a nation almost single-handedly, but today he too is being dismissed as a racist and imperialist. The context in which his leadership flourished (a world at war) has long ago disappeared.

For anyone thinking about what it takes to become a great leader — and how important context is — it may be worthwhile to remember that prior to the rise of Winston Churchill, it was then prime minister Joseph Chamberlain who was hailed by a relieved public as a national hero for avoiding war with Germany when he met with Hitler in 1939. It was only months later, when Hitler showed his true colours, that the public took its collective revenge on Chamberlain's leadership by rejecting him. No longer was he revered as the nation's hero, and Munich would forever be a metaphor for cowardly appeasement.

The context had changed. In Munich's aftermath, meanwhile, Churchill, conventionally criticized for his hawkish belligerence, suddenly was being hailed for his clear-eyed clairvoyance, hailed as someone who had the right stuff for a nation in crisis. Chamberlain, loved by the public for taking steps to prevent Britain's entry in a catastrophic European war, had become the whipping boy for appeasement. What had changed between 1939 and 1945? In terms of culture, not much. What had changed dramatically was context, which is why it's worth remembering that fresh off the Allied victory in 1945, Churchill almost immediately fell out of favour with a public weary of war by appearing to advocate a new war against Britain's ally Russia. Same Churchill, the same Brits ... different context. Politics is a business in at least one sense: a change in context can push a leader through the inevitable three acts generally much faster.

When thinking about leadership, the mistake is ignoring context. It's a three-act play, right? Unfortunately, context cannot be controlled, only managed. In whichever act you may find yourself, having the tools of the right culture in place can help minimize the disruptions caused by context.

Remember:

- Effective culture-driven leadership requires that culture be *identified*.
- We identify with a culture (and with its trajectory). Dissent can weaken culture.
- "We're in this together." Culture should promote a powerful desire for association.

When we talk about culture-driven leadership wanting to create and not destroy, it doesn't mean that we can prevent a business from failing. Not every leaky roof can be patched, and a simple fact of life is that a business has an allotted time span. Businesses fail every day. It's inevitable. Culture-driven leadership is not about doing the impossible or performing miracles. It is about doing whatever can be done to maximize peak performance.

Risk can be explained objectively; it can only be experienced subjectively.

When Elon Musk bought the massively popular social messaging platform Twitter (now X), staffers went ballistic and accused him of committing a kind of cultural genocide at the company. Some believed that the company had become complacent, too comfortable with its own success, too indifferent to its core mission of being a platform for free speech, one not limited to "approved" speech. Others saw a company proud of its dedication to creating a forum for minority voices, wherever they are. What cannot be disputed is that the two perspectives are not aligned. How they might be — and what that will mean — is an interesting leadership challenge.

TALENT IS LIKE COMMON SENSE

God created the world and everything in it in seven days. In today's competitive world, it would have to be three days — tops.

Leadership is commonly associated with creation and innovation; it could be a product, a service, a new technology, or a new way of doing things. It starts with an idea. You might bring in a team of trusted colleagues to map out a game plan. You pitch to investors. Then comes the green light. Now what? You have the idea, the plan, the strategy for execution. Next comes the challenge of finding the talent you need.

It's said that the thing about common sense is how uncommon it is. The same can be said about talent. It's not as easy to find as you might think. The more hiring you do, the more challenges you face finding like-minded, ambitious, and enthusiastic individuals who share your vision and mission. It's often at this point that things become very real and serious for the first time. It was only yesterday you had this crazy idea. Now, you're hiring people who you've sold on your vision; now, they are depending on you to make it happen. From here, the risk becomes exponential, since every person added to the effort will have their own interpretation of the company mission and will have their own sense of their role. The focused *explicit* mission you created is suddenly expanded, diluted, and twisted to suit individual interests. Talk about herding cats!

What to do? How do you manage this common aspect of creating a new business? What principles should you judge prospects on? How flexible should you be? How is the "hire slow, fire fast" principle applied? And, most important, what setbacks would you accept if they do not fit with the mission or the culture of the business? The business always needs to move quickly. How can you do this with hiring? Any shortcuts?

Whenever I've chatted with colleagues about former decisions, I'm surprised how often I'm asked why I failed to fire so-and-so sooner. The person in question was resented, for example, as not being a team player or was seen as working against the grain. "Everyone knew this, but you were so slow to get rid of them. How come?"

Well, I probably *didn't know*. Not at first. Most likely I was too busy with other priorities* and not focused enough on what I should have been. A leader needs to have a broad "touch all the bases" approach. I focused on the idea of being able to read people and culture and seeing the big picture. Finding that perspective "above the clouds." I learned a lesson. I zeroed in on perfecting my hiring strategies. I made it a point to never hire anyone who didn't "fit" the personality and character profile of the company. You can easily change what you do, it's almost impossible to change who you are. As I have said, firing a person is not their mistake, but mine. The "create and not destroy" mindset is about giving "right fit" people an opportunity to flourish.

ONE SIZE DOES NOT FIT ALL

Leadership choices are often based on what it takes to get the job done. I have had the privilege to lead several startups in my career (including Aqua Australis, ING Direct, and Zenbanx). With each, the focus was *primarily* on growth and creating a new business to make profits and build value. At Deak International, I was CEO of a turnaround operation. The focus was to save the business (it had fallen into bankruptcy), create stability, and maintain the value of its core assets. I also had an opportunity to wind down a business (North American Trust). The primary focus in that job was to save brand value and protect jobs and depositors. What each had in common was *the opportunity to demonstrate leadership*; in other words, to "win the day."

What's important to keep in mind is that each job demanded a *bespoke* leadership style. I, as the leader, needed to adjust and adapt my style to meet specialized circumstances. It's like being the only actor in a five-actor play and having to play all the parts (and serve as director). Performance in each role, by the way, is measured differently, and each has a completely different goal or different *aspect* of success. Understanding the three-act framework and that each demands a tailoring of leadership approach helped me focus

---

* Any leader will tell you that problems can turn themselves into priorities in seconds. It can happen for dozens of reasons (simple or "forgivable" neglect being a big reason). As we have seen, leaders routinely have to juggle priorities, which (obviously) is very hard to do. A time-management paradox for any leader is that when problems arrive at your desk, they are already priorities. Most of us are familiar with being able to "pass a problem" up the ladder. The leader doesn't have that option.

on the *drivers to succeed*. It also forced me to rethink how I approached team-building (the casting-the-play requirement): what skills were required, what behaviours, and what culture was needed to fit the mission and the goal.

We've discussed self-awareness and self-knowledge as indispensable tools in the leadership toolbox. Your degree of self-knowledge (your strengths, weaknesses, and so on) will go a long way helping you to orient yourself in the three-act framework. Some leaders are great with Act I, others with Acts II and III. It's hard to master all three. Chances are, you haven't thought about leadership in this way. Take an Elon Musk. Does he have the personality for Act III leadership?

At one point in my career, I was a mid-level manager in a very big Canadian bank in Toronto. The time had come for the year-end performance review; every manager had to write up their performance results and submit a score, adding comments comparing the year's performance against the last year's results. The dreaded KPIs (key performance indicators). All was going well; I had the wrap-up interview with my boss, who was very complimentary. When he turned over my evaluation to sign, I noticed a comment he had appended: "He [me] tends to intimidate intellectually and challenge his peers." I asked him what this meant.

Each job demanded a *bespoke* leadership style.

"Well, you tend to make your peers feel uncomfortable." It was nothing "too critical," he said, "but it would help morale and teamwork if you were *a bit less intense*. Tone the debates down a bit."

I had no idea that my enthusiasm was being received by my colleagues and co-workers in this way. I decided to be the good team player, however, and "tone it down."

The following year, I faced yet another performance review. This time, however, I was working at a new job — on Wall Street. I had only six months under my belt. I had really wanted to impress, so I was deflated when the comments were good but not great. For instance, "Hit the ground running" was pretty good, but "results were met" seemed *meh*. My boss sat me down and jumped right to the point. "We know you're just getting rolling, but in asking around, the main comment is that you're a bit reserved and not very aggressive or intense. You know the culture here. Get it done. No obstacle too big."

I almost exploded with disbelief. My former boss had advised me to tone it down! My new boss was reprimanding me for not turning up the volume! Bay Street versus Wall Street. It wasn't me; at least, not exactly. *It was the culture and environment that had changed.* The issue was which version of me worked best in the prevailing culture. Different needs, different culture ... different style. It was an incredibly important leadership lesson that I never forgot.

How easily can you recognize not only a different culture but what the needs, norms, and expectations of that new culture are? To succeed, you have to adapt to the environment you find yourself in and foreground the characteristics that best suit the moment. Nobody really wanted "me." They wanted what was needed on the team and what "fit in." It was clear to me that the path to leadership required a certain amount of acting, and trust and commitment were only given to those who played the expected role. Everyone on the team has to be on side and rowing together.*

As a leader I needed to balance being different enough to stand out but familiar enough too, so others would not see me as a threat or as someone who didn't fit into the culture. It's a tough balancing act. It's critical to succeed. Be a chameleon of sorts yet remain the authentic you. It's not easy to do.

LEADERSHIP STYLE: A JACK WELCH STORY

These days, leadership styles seem to be in vogue as long as fashion and fads. What's in one year is out the next. For instance, Nobel Prize–winning economist Milton Friedman's philosophy that emphasized private profits

---

* But doesn't this undermine everything I have said earlier about "not fitting in"? No, not at all. Here's why: the goal is not to "fit in." It's a question of strategy. The goal is to get it done. What's important is how you define "it." What are you trying to get done? The other stuff is strategy. For instance, if I want to be accepted by a group of conservative Englishmen, I don't go into the room bragging about hockey or criticizing the poor quality of British poutine. The same is true in any situation. It's all about the winning performance.

over public responsibility dominated leadership thinking in the 1970s. Jack Welch, the "Manager of the Century," according to *Fortune* magazine, defined for the 1980s what it meant to succeed in business. "What he created at GE became the way companies now operate."[5] Today, the emphasis has shifted from profit and share value to happiness and self-value, self-fulfillment, remote workplace options, increased flexibility, et cetera.

What will it mean to be a leader in a future where, more and more, the workplace culture is being dictated by bottom-up decision-making? Perhaps what's in vogue now won't be so favourably looked on in the future; perhaps we'll see a slow transition back to something that more resembles the profit-driven top-down leadership styles Friedman championed.*

Leadership styles come and go; the need for leaders does not. Don't confuse leaders with leadership. Jack Welch was without question a dynamic force in leadership; during his tenure, he transformed GE "into the most valuable company in the world, groomed a flock of protégés who went on to run major companies of their own, and set the standard by which other C.E.O.s were measured." It's a legacy that continues to dominate business leadership even after his death in 2022. "He exerted a powerful and lasting influence on American business, informing how workers are treated, how shareholders are rewarded and how C.E.O.s comport themselves in an increasingly divisive age." Our world is what "Jack Welch helped create." As business writer David Gelles wrote in a recent profile, Welch's value as a leader was evidenced by how dramatically the fortunes of the company dropped after his retirement; he described the company as going into a "tailspin from which it would never recover." In fact, without Welch at the controls, GE management "admitted defeat" and announced that the company "would be broken up for good."

> **Leadership styles come and go; the need for leaders does not.**

---

* We saw a perfect example of this recently when in his purchase of the social media giant X (Twitter) Elon Musk demanded that, among other things, X employees prepare themselves for working much longer hours or resign. The proposal did not go over well.

"In the decades since Mr. Welch assumed power," Gelles wrote, "the economy at large has come to resemble his skewed priorities. Wages [have] stagnated and jobs [have] moved overseas. C.E.O. pay went stratospheric, and buybacks and dividends boomed. Factories closed and companies found ways to pay fewer taxes.

"Beyond his enduring influence on the economy," Welch "redefined what it meant to be a boss" by "personifying an aggressive, materialistic style of management that endures to this day." He characterizes the "Welch way": a "ruthless devotion to maximizing short-term profits at any cost." Welch "closed factories and fired employees by the tens of thousands, unleashing a series of mass layoffs that destabilized the American working class. He devised systems like 'stack ranking,' which mandated that the bottom 10 percent of workers be fired each year and took root at other companies. And he embraced offshoring and outsourcing, sending labor overseas and turning to other companies to provide back-office functions like accounting and printing."

Huge profits, absolutely, "but the ways [Welch] created so much shareholder value often did more harm than good." According to one CEO cited by Gelles, "A lot of GE leaders were thought to be business geniuses. But they were just cost-cutters. And you can't cost-cut your way to prosperity." Gelles concludes: "Welch's influence on American business continues to this day, informing how workers are treated, how shareholders are rewarded and how C.E.O.s comport themselves *in an increasingly divisive age*" (my emphasis).

It seems to me the days of the Milton Friedmans and Jack Welches are over. It's even a question how much longer a Musk or Zuckerberg can escape a serious correction or reckoning.

Of course, their fall would be our fall, too. Technological innovations and our global economy have created an interconnectedness that is profound. As a result, any disturbance in one part of the world, one part of the economy, has repercussions everywhere. A seismic change along any of the fault lines can produce a tsunami far away. This situation has never existed before. A leadership style that fails to recognize this can destroy an economy in its effort to maximize profits. The spirit of "we are here to create, not destroy" is about the important *broader mission* that should be pushing us to succeed. The success achieved can be measured in a number of ways; *success cannot be* consistently reduced to cutting costs or maximizing profits.

What's important here is not the leadership style of Jack Welch. Each of us in our own way is a product of the culture we inhabit and influenced by the shapers (to different degrees) of that culture; the two are hard to separate. The culture Jack Welch created at GE had its lifespan, as all cultures do. Each is replaced by a succeeding culture. On and on. Academics study business cultures and draw conclusions, but it's not clear what help that might be to leaders in the here and now. Or in the world of "what's coming next." As we will discuss in a later chapter, the biggest challenge for any leader is to *endure*: to make leadership meaningful and relevant across an endless series of confrontational ups and downs. Jack Welch could do well what his successors could not, and that is interesting and perhaps instructive.[*]

> The biggest challenge for any leader is to *endure*: to make leadership meaningful and relevant.

What did he know that they didn't? Perhaps they just didn't recognize that a new context had emerged and that it created new leadership needs and standards? Paraphrasing a question we asked at the very beginning of this book, did Welch's leadership style create more problems than it solved?

TRUST YOUR INSTINCTS

My own career illustrates that leadership lessons can come early or late in the journey. And that is true for all leaders. Context is always in play, challenging what we take for granted about leadership. I hear people being told all the time that when in doubt "trust your instincts." And then I see them

---

[*] It's the proximity to power problem: leaders who are too much in the mould of their predecessor or not differentiated enough often are like the second generation who inherits — and squanders — an a fortune. (By the way, this doesn't in any way undermine the value of mentoring. It reveals something more fundamental about what is needed from a leader.)

making incredibly dumb decisions or taking ill-advised actions. When millions of years ago we all lived in caves and hunted and gathered for our survival, trusting our instincts made sense. After all, what else was there? Today it's much different. We don't need our instincts to survive. Most of us do not face daily threats to our survival. Far from it, in fact. So where does that leave us?

Unlike much else in life, effective leadership depends heavily on instinct.

I remember, for instance, when I was a senior in high school being assigned an English essay on Shakespeare's *Hamlet*. I put together a very elaborate schematic and description of the play, its plot, characters, and themes. I remember being very proud of the result and anticipated a good grade. A few weeks later, the teacher handed back the reports and I ended up with a D. The only reason I did not fail outright, the teacher said, was that I had put in so much effort. It was a gut punch. The essay was criticized for being "confusing," "rambling," "without structure." And this: "Simple-mindedness is not the same thing as simplicity."

I remember the comment word-for-word just because it was so brutal and *unfair*. A few years later in university, I was enrolled in an English literature class and was reading Milton's *Paradise Lost* when I started thinking about my *Hamlet* paper. To be honest, I was still brooding about it. *Was it really that bad?* I decided to ask my English professor if he would have a look at the report and give me some feedback and any perspective that he thought might help. He agreed. (I knew that he would also see my high-school teacher's comment and grade in the report, of course, but I figured I had nothing to lose.) About a week later, the professor stopped me in the hallway and asked if I had a few minutes. Yes, of course, I was anxious to hear his comments. The high-school teacher really did not understand what I was attempting to achieve with the assignment, he said. The teacher's criticism was "too linear." No wandering off the prescribed path. No digressions: stick verbatim to the assignment as directed. My professor, on the other hand, appreciated my unorthodox approach; the result was unique, unexpected, and informative. Had I written the same paper for his class, he would have given it an A.

The point here is not that my high-school teacher was wrong. And the boss I had who suggested I "tone it down" wasn't wrong either. We have all had moments — perhaps quite a few — when others just didn't get it. It's normal. The challenge in leadership, however, is getting over the "they just didn't get it" mindset to developing a "what do they need and how can I deliver it" mindset. It's all about the context. What is expected, and what will work to secure the desired outcome? Today, I would look at what my high-school teacher "wanted" and figure out a way to say what I wanted to say while staying inside the guardrails. Not ignoring them but figuring out a way perhaps to move them a bit. An actor cannot play the part of Prince Hamlet in the same voice or character one would a Barnardo or Francisco. The approach needs to be adjusted and adapted to the outcome. One has to hold one's own counsel, yes, but one has to adjust one's leadership style to fit the circumstances. It's personal and emotional, but it's the nature of many things in our daily lives. The key lesson for me was that one has to be really self-aware and good at making leadership fit the situation. There are no time-outs. One has to be authentic and consistent. It's a practised art form and yes it can be done.

I still have that report today. I pull it out once in a while and smile.

WHY ALL THIS MATTERS

Leadership can be an ugly business, but it is needed. During the U.S. Civil War, for example, the U.S. general Ulysses Grant was much criticized for the high casualty rates his troops suffered. President Abraham Lincoln defended him, however, and offered the general the following blunt advice: "Hold on with a bulldog grip, and chew and choke as much as possible." *Get it done.*

There will always be times when leadership demands more than what we have to offer, or skills that we don't have, or skills we have that are not an appropriate fit. There is no such thing as a leadership "one size fits all." Context matters.

Creating is hard work. Preserving what has been created — keeping it fresh and meaningful — is even harder. We all have three acts. The important role of any leader is making each act count. We here to create, not destroy.

CONCLUDING THOUGHT

Management is important, but it's different from leadership. The focus of management is the successful carrying out of a set of defined tasks. Leadership addresses (increasingly in real time) how the vision is defined and why. Leadership today has to make quicker decisions with less information. Inevitably, each piece of information acquires more importance and has a much larger impact on the outcome and consequences. It always raises the stakes. Success or failure is *the* leadership metric.

ACTION POINTS

- Success is seasonal. What's "new" and "popular" in spring could be "yesterday's news" by fall. Timing is always impacted by context.
- Effective culture-driven leadership requires that culture be identified and described.
- We identify with a culture. It's always personal. It stands for the need to belong.
- Metastasized dissent will always weaken culture.
- "We're in this together" culture promotes a powerful desire for membership and shared investment in outcomes.
- Always make time to focus on the core aspects of culture. It will evolve on its own unless you influence it.
- Every business has three acts: birth, maturity, death. Some businesses are destined to die faster than others. Leadership needs often change from one stage to the next.
- Context means problems will not appear "pre-packaged" and "off the shelf," which means leaders and leadership styles are often the offspring of context.

Chapter 3

WE WILL CONSTANTLY LEARN

There is a lot we don't know, and we have to be open to being curious. This is especially true for the culture-driven leader. You must always be learning new ways and innovating to do better. Everything is up for questioning. The culture-driven leader always has to have a receptive mindset. We don't use the phase "It's the way things are always done here!" Judgments and decisions have to be made. And what's "new" is not always what's "best."

Many life lessons come early in the journey; some much later.

. . .

Of a recent world leader, it was said, "He doesn't really know anything, which is forgivable. But he also doesn't want to know anything, which isn't." What's being said is that a key foundational cornerstone of effective leadership is a healthy curiosity. I would also say that — in general — a healthy curiosity keeps ego in check and that keeps one humble.

If you think you're the most important person in the room, you aren't.

It's an interesting fact that ground-breaking work in the field of mathematics is rarely done by those over the age of thirty.* It may be that challenging orthodoxy and upending conventional thinking is much easier when one is young, ambitious, eager, open to opportunity and new ways of thinking, and — critically — *uninvested* in the status quo. Smashing taboos is what gets one noticed and makes a reputation and, in turn, a career. Having *been noticed*, however, and having made a name and reputation, the innovator faces the challenge of shifting their behaviour from *offending* the status quo to *defending* it. The early Picasso was an affront to art; the later Picasso set records for sales. The rebel, in other words, inevitably ends up as the new establishment.

The age of the average CEO in 2017 was fifty. That's an increase of five years from 2012, when the average age was forty-five.[1] The reason, according to one survey, was that since more (and increasingly diverse) responsibilities and liabilities were being taken on by CEOs, "a greater premium [was being placed] on experience and judgment."[2]

> The rebel inevitably ends up as the new establishment.

The average tenure of a CEO is about eight years (7.6).[3] Interestingly, the "optimal" length of tenure, according to a major scientific study, is only 4.8 years![4] In time, the study warns, a CEO can grow "less attuned to market conditions and customers." The more invested a CEO becomes in the position and the outcome, the more risk-averse they will be. "They favor avoiding losses over pursuing gains. Their attachment to the status quo makes them less responsive to vacillating consumer preferences."[5] The longer the CEO remains at the helm, "the more likely they are to stop reacting to market conditions and their customers' desires, ultimately hurting the firm's performance." By not challenging the status quo — by playing it safe — the complacent

---

* "I want to stress the importance of being young and technical. Young people are just smarter. Why are most chess masters under 30?" asked Facebook founder and CEO Mark Zuckerberg in 2017. It's a fair point. Youth may have an advantage in some industries and enterprises focused entirely on innovation. It becomes an interesting question whether young entrepreneurs like Zuckerberg will evolve into outstanding leaders.

CEO risks "further alienating [themselves] from market environments and weakening customer relations, which in the end hurt" the company's "overall performance."

The solution to this problem is not to simply terminate a CEO as soon as they hit the 4.8-years-in-tenure mark. What does the study recommend? "If company boards restructure CEO packages *to cater to consumers more*, you may find yourself with better results." Does that sound familiar?

In this chapter, we will explore what "we will constantly learn" means and its implications for culture-driven leadership.

CUSTOMER-FOCUSED LEARNING

The U.S. Constitution requires a president be at least thirty-five years of age.* Only ten of forty-six presidents were under fifty when their terms began. Thirteen have been sixty or over, and all of that group have served since Harry Truman was in office (1945–1953). Presidents Biden and Trump both entered office as the oldest presidents in history. Joe Biden will be eighty-one if re-elected in 2024; Donald Trump, seventy-eight. A prospective voter was asked about the ages of the candidates in a *New York Times* article in July 2022. "How are you going to accurately lead your country if your mind is *still stuck* 50, 60 or 70 years ago?" the voter wondered. "It's not the same, and people aren't the same, and your old ideas aren't going to work as well anymore."[6]

The world keeps changing, and everything in that world changes as well, right? But that isn't news. When has this ever *not been* true? The world has changed more (and in more sweepingly fundamental ways) in the last ten years than in the last two hundred or more. The point being made by the voter is this: a powerful perception exists *out there* that leaders of a certain age and mindset either *won't be* or *aren't capable of changing and adapting.* Is it true? That doesn't matter: it's the perception that counts. It's what the voter thinks. Once again: it's what the customer or consumer thinks that matters.

---

* Thirty-five seems young but remember the life expectancy for the average Colonial-era male was around thirty-eight. Members of the elite, of course, could expect to live longer. George Washington was sixty-seven when he died. Jefferson and Adams were well over eighty, as was Benjamin Franklin.

Age is just one of many potential separators we have to deal with in our increasingly globalized world. Closing your mind off to all that change is not an option; hoping you can autopilot your leadership to the outcome is not realistic. If the customer doesn't believe you are "hearing" them and their concerns and acting in timely and meaningful ways to address those concerns, you will be held accountable.

A REBEL WITH A CAUSE?

In the classic movie *The Wild One*, Marlon Brando plays the discontented leader of a biker gang. "What are you rebelling against?" he is asked.

"What d'ya got?"

It's a great line, but not the mindset of a *culture-driven* leader. Disruption without direction is a dead end. Why are we doing it this way? Is there a better way? How do we create better value for our customer? Great questions! As we know, context keeps changing and that means the answers to these questions need to be updated and refreshed continually. Let's call it being a rebel *with a cause*. It's fun to talk about revolutionizing an industry. We did it with ING Direct. But once you've broken down the walls of the Bastille and set a spark to the revolution, the difficult job for leadership is actually building the better society.

> **Disruption without direction is a dead end.**

LEADING A TEAM

It may be obvious but being curious and open to learning involves both the mind and emotions. You cannot recognize and take advantage of emergent opportunities, come up with good ideas, create customer interest and loyalty, solve problems, or be an agent of positive change if you are siloed within you own closed mindset, are uncurious, refuse to ask questions, avoid challenges, or are unable or unwilling to identify gaps, omissions, points of friction, asymmetries, or misalignments that threaten desired outcomes. You can't lead if you don't engage with your team.

It sounds corny, but do you mostly get along with people? Can you recognize and empathize with what people around you are experiencing and going through? We were all children once. How satisfied were you with the "because I said so" parental response? Being open mentally and emotionally doesn't mean — it shouldn't mean — wasting time trying to be everybody's friend. You need to be respected. You also need to make sure people feel *valued*.

Leaders have to be humble and confident enough to understand and learn. You're the leader, but you are still a member of a team. Hierarchies need to be respected and preserved, but only to the extent of reinforcing the culture and the mission. It's incumbent upon leaders to create a culture that supports learning. Encouraging open questioning that is designed to come up with better solutions and breakthroughs in established practices is a winning and

> **Leaders have to be humble and confident enough to understand and learn.**

positive experience, if it's allowed to happen. What matters is not who comes up with the idea, who has the most seniority, who's the smartest, the loudest, who has the most experience or the best resumé. Traditional hierarchies need to be ignored: the focus should be on collaboration and teamwork. This requires transparency, authenticity. The input needs to be acknowledged and genuinely considered. It's a principle of transparency in a company culture.*

Making constant learning part of the culture will motivate and drive the culture toward the desired outcome. The organization becomes a rebel with a cause. It's a state of mind that sees the state of how things are and wonders,

---

* It's important to remember, however, that decision-making needs to be structured so as to maintain the integrity of collaborative- and teamwork-focused leadership. Everyone needs to have their say, but decisions are not communal. Once a decision is made, it's final. The time for further discussion and input is over. At that point, it's "everyone on board" time.

realizes, it's not enough, that wants to make it better. Do you as a culture-driven leader believe that at a foundational level every single thing one does can be done better? I'm sure every day you are confronted with things that you immediately feel can be done better! Leadership requires staying open and receptive to better ways of doing things. Not necessarily newer. *Better*. And where does a leader find the source of "better"?

Disruption is never easy, in business especially; it's incredibly tempting to want things to run as smoothly as possible. As a leader, of course, you are ultimately responsible for everything that happens under your watch, so the temptation is to engineer the leadership job description to focus on limited outcomes (for instance, a focus on profit or growth to the exclusion of all else); leaders might be tempted to ignore or distance themselves from sources of disruption in the hopes that the problem might go away. It can work ... in the short term ... but eventually context will always catch up and leaders will find themselves once again in the crosshairs.

A culture-driven leader deals with the pressure by having an open mind. The philosopher Socrates was famous for a method of inquiry that focused on doubt as a necessary first step in achieving true wisdom. He challenged his companions to question what they thought they knew. How do we know what we think we know? How can we be certain? Are we just making assumptions? Behaving like zombies stumbling around in a "trance of action."[7] The thing is, we depend on the shared norms of behaviour for most of what we do; in fact, society could not function without them. The problem for a leader arises when the patterns of orthodox behaviour take over, and we act without really knowing why we are doing what we do. The philosopher John Stuart Mill called these too-familiar habits of mind "the magical influence of custom."

"I KNOW WHAT I'M DOING. WHAT COULD POSSIBLY GO WRONG?"

BlackBerry was once the gold standard in smartphone technology. What happened? For one thing, company leadership refused to acknowledge what turned out to be a profound change of context; leadership downplayed and dismissed emerging challenges and neglected to take the steps necessary to remain innovative. In short, executives were not interested in learning what was new. By the time the company reacted, it was too late. As one business report concluded, "They executed the loss of market leadership with impressive speed."[8]

THE LEADERSHIP ACHILLES HEEL

Ninety percent of leaders make the same mistake: "I'm in charge. This is what we should be doing." Eventually, maybe, they'll get around to the complex of issues that in all likelihood were the source of the problems and misalignments in the first place. I hope that I can convince aspirational leaders that before you get into what *should be done*, get to a place "above the clouds" where you see what *needs to be done*. Ask questions! Find out what is going on. If you have the right culture in place, you will find out. A healthy culture will have feedback loops that allow critical input to circulate. But don't leave it at that. Ask questions. And act! That is the heart and soul of culture-driven leadership: prioritizing the culture. It will help you decide what it is that can be done.

> A healthy culture will have feedback loops that allow critical input to circulate.

LEADERSHIP IS A POP QUIZ EVERY DAY

As a leader, I try to put my own skills to the test every day. It might be like walking to the edge of a very high cliff, and asking yourself, "Do I have what it takes to survive this fall? How do I know? Are there new things I could be doing that would improve my chances?"

You take the risk in order to keep the culture vibrant and meaningful. Take the inspirational poster off the wall; you need to be seen living it.

YOUTH OR EXPERIENCE?

It shouldn't come down to a choice between youth and experience. You need both. And by both, I mean that as a leader one must be open and willing to try new things — the kind of adaptive and experiential characteristics we associate with youth — but have the experience and maturity to examine, judge, filter, and organize things. Being open-minded is not the same thing as being open to anything. A leader needs to know how and when to establish limits.

Consider that 70 percent of American workers believe "they can do their boss's job more effectively."[9] The younger you are in the workplace, the more likely you are to feel you can outperform your boss. What this should be telling us (at a minimum) is that pressure is increasing on leaders to achieve top performance — not just for right now but year after year. Otherwise, that optimal 4.8 years of tenure quoted above will shrink ever further.

Experience should be thought of as a resource that needs to be constantly revised and replenished. It isn't merely the cumulative weight of experience that counts, which is why context is so important. Experience by itself can be just like a worn-out set of instructions for a machine that no longer exists (like a booklet on how to program a VCR). On the other hand, absent experience, the sell-by date on youth is tomorrow. A great leader needs to be aware of the value of both.

The person who leads a successful protest may not be the best choice when it comes to success at the bargaining table. For instance, Greta Thunberg was only fifteen when she began challenging the governments of the world to take more decisive action on climate change. Her youth, her idealism, and her outspokenness have resonated. Is she, however, an effective leader? Or is she more effective as a catalyst for action? Whatever one may think, it's clearly true that many look to her to lead the movement for action on climate change. On the other hand, when war was declared in 1939, Britain turned to an experienced leader, Winston Churchill, sixty-five at the time, the conventional age for retirement. His experience and temperament were seen to be what was needed in a leader. Different times and different circumstances often demand different sources of leadership. In any case, effective leadership is always required, whatever the context.

Age might be relevant when innovations and discoveries are all that matter. A revolutionary genius like Albert Einstein was essentially tapped out by the time he was thirty, and the mature period of his career was devoted mainly to defending his theories and fending off challenges from younger physicists.

It could also be argued that had Einstein followed the traditional career path of young physicists by entering the university system with all the other graduate students of his generation, he might not have made the groundbreaking discoveries he did. As it was, Einstein spent most of his twenties completely outside the world of academia, working alone in a patent office in Switzerland. It was during this period, in 1905 to be precise, that he had his *annus mirabilis*, producing his theories of relativity (special and general), his study of the photoelectric effect (for which he won the Nobel Prize), and two other ground-breaking papers. Mark Zuckerberg dropped out of college in 2004 at the age of twenty to start up Facebook. Had he not done so, it's fun to wonder if he might have ended up working for Facebook (or something similar) rather than running it.

THERE'S NO SUCH THING AS OFF-THE-RACK LEADERSHIP

The world changes and we all change with it. The older we get the more likely it is we have committed to habits and behaviours that are hard to break. Young adulthood is — or it should be — by nature a period of rebellion, of pushing boundaries and challenging customs and orthodoxies. Being new to something when you are, in fact, new to it is not an achievement. It's just the way it is. Embracing a "we are new here" mindset from the beginning of one's apprenticeship to the flowering of one's career and even beyond is a real achievement. And that mental mindset dovetails with the "we will constantly learn" bias.

Again, let's ask: What kind of a leadership is possible for you? Leaders I have known in my own career, as well as leaders I admire from history, all have one thing in common: a confidence tempered by humility. The leaders I respect have all had experience with failures and setbacks but have found ways for dealing with and overcoming failure. *They learn from their mistakes and missteps.* Trust me, it isn't easy admitting you've screwed up. Even harder, however, is having the humility to realize you need to keep learning. Realizing that you don't know it all and having the open-mindedness to learn from a setback and see it as an invaluable learning opportunity.

Learning from your own experience (and mistakes) is good. Learning from the experience (and mistakes) of your colleagues is good too. But a real commitment to learning requires looking beyond the world around you, seeing insight from far and wide.

The average age of a tech worker at two of the largest U.S. firms is twenty-eight. It makes sense, of course. Young people are far more likely to be receptive to technology since it's what they've grown up with. With such a homogeneous workforce, there is a danger of tech companies becoming too much of a tribe composed of too many of the like-minded. Where is the diversity? Who are the sources of disruption? Are they being listened to? When I was in banking, I used to refuse employee requests to attend banking conferences. Why are you expecting to hear something new and different at a conference for bankers organized by financial services vendors? Get outside your tribe. Get outside your comfort zone. Challenge what you think you know by actually being somewhere where you don't know anything or anyone and have to be curious and learn and adapt.

> **Learning from your own experience (and mistakes) is good. Learning from the experience (and mistakes) of your colleagues is good, too.**

All of that new is good, but it's essential to ensure that all that is useful from the new and different gets integrated. The rest should be cast aside. What's important is for all to buy into the new that's accepted. We are by nature members of tribes; we can't help it. The challenge facing leaders today is that there are so many sources of fragmentation that can challenge any attempt to define who (and who is not) a member of the tribe, and — most critical — what keeps them all under one umbrella. A culture-driven leader's job is learning how to create meaningful rules of broader membership that can overcome narrower tribal loyalties. A leader committed to fostering a "we are always learning" culture — the leader whose behaviour reinforces the learning paradigm ("we're always learning ... and that includes me!") — minimizes the corrosive consequences of damaging dissent by providing creative civil forums.

"THIS SHOULD WORK" IS NOT AN OPTION

Earlier, I said that a leader needs to create certainty. In the technology world, one often hears "this should work!" It's hard to imagine any other sector that could get away with knowingly releasing products with defects, as is common in the software industry. Can you imagine stepping into the cabin of a modern passenger airplane and the pilot calling back, "We should be fine. This plane *should* fly." As we know, when we say something *should* work, it's understood that the outcome is expected but not certain, but rarely do we really consider the implications of that situation. It's just casually said and accepted. We need certainty, but few things are certain in practice. I've now seen this "should" in other businesses like health care and construction.

SPOTLIGHT: LEADERSHIP

The value of emotional intelligence

Remember as a teenager when you would do something dumb, and your parents would look at you as if you had just lit your hair on fire? *What were you thinking?*

We all want to know what people around us are thinking. It's a universal human trait. We see a friend smile and we are pleased; we see a frowning boss and are worried. Emotional intelligence (EI) is a metric used to measure how good we are at reading correctly the emotions of others. EI "can have a surprisingly powerful effect on our lives, from our ability to foster long-term relationships with friends and romantic partners to whether we're able to succeed in school and pursue meaningful work that gives us a sense of purpose."[10]

I'd say that about 80 percent of my success as a leader has been due to the people I have been able to recruit, and that is a direct consequence of high EI skills. Generally, EI is the ability to empathize, but it can be broken down to four key elements[11]:

- self-awareness
- self-regulation
- social awareness
- conflict management skills

The earlier in your leadership trajectory you come to terms with the powerful utility of EI the better. Think about EI practically as a difference between judgements and decision-making. For instance, leaders are expected to make countless decisions. What isn't remarked on often enough is how often (and how important it is to the culture) a leader needs to make a judgment. What's the difference? Deciding to have a water instead of an orange soda at lunch is a decision. Simple. It's short-term and based entirely on personal preference. Banning a vending machine because sugar-flavoured drinks are unhealthy and replacing it with sugar-free drinks and healthy snacks is a judgment. It has long-term impact and is made for the collective best interests of the group. Generally, decisions are technical: they relate to economy and efficiency (what will work for the outcome). Judgments are aesthetic: they reinforce the culture by defining why it's the right way to achieve the outcome.

> **The foundational first principle when it comes to culture-driven leadership is self-awareness.**

In my experience, the foundational first principle when it comes to culture-driven leadership is self-awareness. Without it, the others are difficult to achieve and impossible to maintain over the long term.* What follows

---

* Consider the case of Howard Schultz. He appeared genuinely shocked by the revolt of Starbucks employees. He shouldn't have been. Not being able to see what needs to be seen is an example of leadership self-awareness deficit.

are a series of ten brief but I think important starting points for how to think about what self-awareness might mean in everyday leadership.

It's not just about skills

Timing is key in so many things. In leadership it can be decisive. To be self-aware is not very helpful unless one is aware also of one's surroundings (culture) and the forces (internal and external) that a leader needs to navigate (context). As has been made clear, our globalized economy has increased the pace of change dramatically. Thus, *timing*. It's common knowledge in business that there are three places to find oneself: the leading edge, the cutting edge, and the trailing edge. Prematurely jumping into a market (being the guest who arrives an hour before the party starts), for instance, is just as bad as waiting too long (sorry, the party's over). A leader is looking for the sweet spot where the market is receptive but not too crowded. Makes sense. You need to read people *and* context. Leadership depends on timing.

Learning how to read people is not inherently that different from learning how to read context. It means being aware and "tuned into" the signs, like a meteorologist might be aware of the early signs of a storm. To lead means often to find oneself in uncharted territory, focused on ideas, projects, or products that are novel. It's a good thing to be ahead of the competition, but it's wise to not get too far ahead of the pack. Doing that means that your company will have to bear the cost (money, time, and energy) of researching and developing a product or service that is too far ahead of its time. As I mentioned earlier, when I led a team creating a startup, our desire to be first out of the gate resulted in us pushing too hard. We succeeded, but in succeeding we failed: we arrived too early, which caused drag on the cost-versus-adoption timeline! As we know, being there *too early* results in recognition, yes, but the lion's share of spoils and success probably will go to the followers. History has many examples. Think of pioneers like Gutenberg, Nikola Tesla, Thomas Edison, and Alexander Graham Bell. *Too late*, of course, is just, well, too late. No more slices of pie. A leader needs to be at the front of change, but not on the bleeding edge. Don't get ahead too far; don't pile on at the end. It's timing that counts when getting to market. It sounds easy but experience suggests that it's very hard to do.

If you want to be forgiven, find a priest

The leader has in the end the sole responsibility to get it done. It's not a forgiving dynamic. It's success or failure; it's objective, not subjective. No one will give you a pass for failing. Meaning: having the absolute best team around you and having them be able to do the best work they can is a must. A leader with high marks when it comes to qualities like empathy knows how to build and to sustain a team. A leader without high marks on self-awareness will never build a good team. Not over the long term, anyway.

The most difficult leadership attribute today is self-reflection

Think the title, the salary, the nice car, and the fancy office on the top floor will immunize you from disaster? Leaders *literally* are faced with earning the leadership role every day. If you don't have a good handle on who you are and what you can accomplish, you are handicapped. Have a realistic view of yourself. You'll be respected for it.

Your cowboy boots are a size too small

An effective leader needs to be the first out front when it comes to judgment. It could be of a project, a potential innovation, a new opportunity, a new hire, whatever. What are the upsides? What are the downsides? You have to make the final decision. Often, thinking can default to the overly cautious: "Oh, no, that will never work." Is it true? Or is it a case of risk-aversion? I've had so many conversations over the years that very quickly went negative, and the focus shifted to all the things that could go wrong. I came up with a challenge. "Your cowboy boots are too small!" At first, they were puzzled. "Cowboys love big open spaces," I explained.

In other words, they were thinking too small. Most got it, some didn't. It just wasn't where they felt comfortable. *It didn't fit*. You want to have people around who like the fit, who aren't afraid of big ideas or thinking about things in a new way.

Make it so!

Remember Captain Jean-Luc Picard from the Star Trek franchise? His default command was "Make it so!" Simple? Not so much. Recent events have made it obvious that thinking can often become *too optimistic*. No one benefits from pretending that doing the difficult thing is simpler than it is. Certainly, the chill that has settled over the Silicon Valley technology sector is a great example of having a pair of cowboy boots that are way too big.

Decisions are like wet cement; they take time to harden

Just because a decision has been made, it doesn't mean that suddenly everyone is on board. Even a unanimous decision can involve varying degrees of acceptance or commitment. Resistance cannot be eliminated by decree; it needs to be dissolved over time. Ideally, not too much time, which is why having the right culture in place is so important. A healthy culture by its nature will minimize sources of asymmetries. But no culture can be completely immunized from dissent, which is increasingly problematic today in our highly divisive times where threats to culture multiply on a daily basis like a deadly virus. It's important to remember that decisions have to be *continually* sold and supported. Yes, over and over again.

HEART VERSUS HEAD? IT'S A NO-BRAINER

Call it EI or intuition or having an instinct for what makes us tick. Experts estimate that EI accounts for 90 percent "of what sets high performers apart from peers with similar technical skills and knowledge." In fact, 71 percent of employers surveyed said they value EI over IQ.[12] High EI is associated with high levels of self-confidence, trustworthiness, integrity, openness to change, a strong drive to achieve, expertise in building and retaining talent, effectiveness in leading change, persuasiveness, expertise in building and leading teams, optimism (even in the face of failure), and service to clients and customers.

Studies also validate that empathy is the most important leadership skill. For instance, 76 percent of those who reported experiencing empathy from their leaders reported being engaged, compared to 32 percent who experienced less empathy. Fifty percent who reported having empathetic leaders judged their workplace inclusive, compared to 17 percent with "less empathetic" leadership. Sixty-one percent of employees with empathetic leaders were more likely to be innovative; employees with less empathetic leaders were only 13 percent likely to be innovative.[13]

High EI individuals are able to address and identify their own emotional states (especially the negative states) and can take action to control them, resulting in high levels of self-confidence and self-knowledge, which can be highly motivational when it comes to leading by example. The leadership with self-discipline, drive, willingness to learn and adapt, and commitment is always directed at the larger goal. It's inspirational.

Consider an Elon Musk. High EI? What about a Richard Branson?

THE "WELL-INVESTED" PROMISE

The culture inside ING Direct, for instance, was weighted heavily toward encouraging everyone at every level to keep learning, to keep asking questions, to keep themselves open and invested in the outcome, to follow the principles, embrace our values, to keep finding new reasons to make the product and process better. I kept reminding them a lot of people were convinced we'd fail, and they would say, "We told you so."

I wanted them to remember that we were on a unique journey. I even made the message explicit in an early video promoting the ING Direct future.

"If you live the values," I said, "and if they're right — if they fit you — then whatever skills you are going to pick up … about human nature, about interactions, about working with people, about building your own skills … they're going to serve you well for the rest of your life. And you'll look back on the time you joined us for the journey and say: those were months and years well invested." I wanted each of them to believe that "it was worth doing," that years later they could say "it was a great time of my life." Did I mean it? Darned right I did. I still do. And if there is only one thing that anyone reading this book should take away it would be this: In whatever you do, make it count. Make it matter.

Because it does.

THE VALUE OF MENTORSHIP

"If I have seen further," Isaac Newton said, "it is by standing on the shoulders of giants." We all need help as leaders. Why? Because we can't do it alone. And we never operate inside a vacuum. We are all part of the unbroken continuum. What we start we take over from someone ahead of us. If we're lucky and we have done our jobs well, what we've created we turn over to a new generation of leaders. We are just renting space here. Never forget that.

In my own experience, I've been very fortunate to have several great mentors. At university, I worked for a professor who over time took a real interest in me and gave me lots of advice. He shared his experience that put me on the path to teach and start new business ventures. Mike Leenders was a professor of procurement at Western University. He started several businesses and wrote business cases. His work was an inspiration, and I always felt I could go to him with any problem. As a teacher, he was objective and had a lot of sound advice. He listened and never judged but helped me walk through the problem.

We are just renting space here. Never forget that.

We benefit in obvious but also in obscure ways from all those who helped us over the years to become leaders. It's incredibly important to remember that we never know where the most important leadership lessons will come from, or from whom they will come. Be open! When opportunity knocks, don't have your headphones on!

I am often asked: Are leaders born or can leadership be learned? I think it's a bit of both. Leadership *qualities* are universal. Some may have their leadership traits encouraged and will be given the opportunity to gain experience and build upon them over time; others may not be given that opportunity, or circumstances may not be aligned in a way that their leadership skills are allowed to develop. But look at climate activist Greta Thunburg. Did anyone see her coming? Did anyone teach her? Give her opportunity? Some leaders seem like naturals; others only become leaders in times of crisis. It's not a question of whether or not you have what it takes; what's important is that you *take what you have* and make the best of yourself.

A very common default for many leaders, however, is complacency. We are just too busy to think about how we could do better or from whom we might get help. Another is pride. I don't need advice. I know what I'm doing.

When you are starting out, it might not be obvious who might serve as a mentor. In my experience, if you are a hard worker, respected both for what you do and who you are (the character issue), you shouldn't worry about finding a mentor. A mentor will find you.

You first need to make yourself worthy of being mentored. Second, you should know your place. Be honest about your skill set and your level of experience; know what you do well and what you need to work on and take advantage of every opportunity to solicit help or assistance from senior people who are familiar with your work. Obviously, be respectful. Their time and willingness to mentor *costs* them.

It's not always easy knowing who you can trust to give you advice. Learning that is a hugely important lesson that no effective leader can afford to ignore. Is the person giving you advice someone you both respect and desire to emulate? Why? If it's just the prestige or power the person has that appeals, you will not be able to learn a valuable leadership lesson from them. What most leaders will tell anyone willing to listen is that no one thinks leaders work very hard. Good leaders have good work habits, and it's these habits and mindsets that you want to adopt and cultivate. Above all.

> **Be generous with your time, knowledge, skills, and experiences.**

It is also important to find a *mission partner*. Most probably, they will be the person you have worked with the longest and with whom you have the deepest bond. It isn't always possible, of course, to have that someone, but it's incredibly helpful if you can. Having a trusted "number two" who has been there when it's been tough and can remind you of what is important can be hugely important. Mentorship, I have discovered, can move in two directions: top down and bottom up. And sideways! A partner and a true friend that knows what your journey is and who can share the same aspirations and desires will help you immeasurably, but it is hard to find that someone. Who would know you better? Give you better advice? Would walk the path with you? Most critical decisions and choices are always better if you can work them through with a partner.

All leaders will have had mentors, and all good leaders will, themselves, serve as mentors. Make yourself available as a mentor — you need to prepare leaders so they can be ready when you pass the torch.

Which we all will. Be generous with your time, knowledge, skills, and experiences. It's what we all owe the future. To keep at it, to keep it all going, and to keep doing the best we can. Learn as much as you can and pass that knowledge along. It's a real leadership legacy.

CONCLUDING THOUGHT

Leadership requires being focused on always learning and always challenging the status quo. To stay ahead, you have to stay relevant, keep wanting to do better, stay true to the mission. For me, running a business is like living a life. How do you want to live? What guides you? It's a question that goes all the way back to Aristotle: What does it mean to live a virtuous life? Aristotle and his contemporaries believed a virtuous life was based on four attributes: prudence, justice, fortitude, and temperance. We know them today as the four cardinal virtues. Times change; context is changing every day. But some things never change. A good leader needs to know what never changes before knowing how to deal what will change.

ACTION POINTS

- There is a lot we don't know, and we have to be open to learning new things; we have to be curious.
- You can't create the right workplace culture just by saying, "I'm the boss"; however, saying it is the best way to preserve the right culture.
- The easiest part of a home renovation is the teardown; building is hard. Be a rebel but be a rebel with a cause! Make it work.
- The culture-driven promise: In whatever you do, make it count. Make it matter.
- Be a person whose habits and attitude make yourself worthy of being mentored.
- Finding a work and mission partner is a huge learning benefit.

Chapter 4

WE WILL LISTEN; WE WILL SIMPLIFY

It's very hard to simplify things. Anything that is easy to understand or can be done easily, without friction or bottlenecks and in a timely manner, is generally liked. The true guide to creating value for any consumer is to simplify their experience. How do we start? By listening. By being open to the full range of feedback generated by the customer (and your employees!). Learning how to tune in to what you need to hear — and tune out what you don't — is a real challenge.

· · ·

Imagine this example. It's been a long day and you're looking forward to stopping at your local tavern for a beer. The backup at the bar is surprisingly deep. You have to wait a long time to order. *What could be taking so long?* Finally, it's your turn. "Where's Dave?" you ask. Dave has been behind the bar forever.

The new guy shrugs. "I'm Jeff."

Well, okay.

You order. He nods, walks away, and comes back with a clipboard and a pen. "You'll have to fill this out first." It's a questionnaire several pages long.

"What's this?"

"Just fill it out, sir."

"But —"

"If you don't fill it out, sir, I can't serve you. Oh, I also need an I.D. — a driver's licence, social security number, and passport. Insurance number, and at least two letters with your home address and preferably your bank account statements and copies of your latest income tax filing."

You're incredulous. "What for?"

"We need to verify you are who you say you are."

"But I know who I am. And so does Dave. I've been coming here for years."

"I understand that, sir. But I don't know you."

Realizing you have no choice, you waste the next twenty minutes filling out boxes and answering questions that seem to have no point and no relationship to the nature of the simple transaction you are trying to complete. The familiar sense of homecoming you generally have at first entering the bar has vanished. You're angry, upset, and — above all — confused. Why is this happening? Why do they need all this? It takes another ten minutes to find the bartender, who appears to have disappeared. Finally, he appears.

"Where's Jeff?"

"I don't know a Jeff. I'm Steve. Can I help you?"

You are so frustrated you want to scream. The system has turned into a robotic, locked process. A real person is there, but he is just a slave to the system. Anyone notice it does not work?

The whole experience has been ruined. You rip up the questionnaire and walk out. At the door you hear a dull grey robotic voice. "Your business is important to us. Come again soon!"

THE SHORTER LETTER PARADOX

You've probably noticed that the world has become incredibly convenient. Tired of climbing stairs? We have apps that will direct you to the nearest escalator. Tired of composing replies to emails? We have apps for that. No time to cook? No time to shop? Not to worry. We're on it. Think of the time, effort, and costs we save! Then why it doesn't feel that way? Why are we so stressed? Why does so much of modern life seem so complicated? This chapter looks at why all this convenience seems to come at such a high cost.

The philosopher Blaise Pascal famously apologized to a friend for writing such a long letter. "Had I the time, it would have been shorter." *Simplifying is hard.* If you happen to be old enough to remember what it used to be like to program a VCR, you'll agree that by comparison most of our modern gadgets are remarkably intuitive. The range of options we have engineered into our smart devices is staggering. We keep adding more ways in which we can work on digital formats. We add more work but don't eliminate tasks to make things work better. What's going on? Why don't all of these new and improved devices, supposedly designed to make life easier, help us to declutter our lives? In other words, why is it so hard to simplify?

With each step forward in that march to the completely intuitive, it seems we risk taking a step or two back ... if often inadvertently and unintentionally. Rather than making life easier, all this convenience causes so much stress. Are we suffering from "convenience fatigue"?

We've all heard of "complexity bias." Basically, when confronted by a simple versus a less-simple choice, we choose the latter. This bias results in people believing that it's "easier" to "face a complex problem than a simple one."* For instance, in an experiment conducted by scientists at the University of Virginia, a majority (59 percent) *ignored* the simpler solution to a model problem in favour of a more complex solution. In another experiment, *80 percent* of participants asked to edit their own essay opted to *add* to the word count rather than cutting and clarifying (a mere 16 percent). As an opinion columnist for Bloomberg concluded, "A lamentable secret of the universe seems to be that it takes enormous effort to simplify, but no effort at all to do the opposite. Put differently, it's easier to add things, even unnecessary ones, than to subtract."[1]

We experience examples of complexity bias every day. The challenge is identifying complexity bias in services and products. Make an effort to not make it part of the customer experience.

---

* When I use the word "simple" I am referring less to an engineered feature than to a measure of overall user-friendliness. In other words, does it meet my needs? Do exactly what I want it to do? Does it come with a steep learning curve? Save me time? Will there be support whenever and wherever I need it? Will it become more complicated over time? And so on.

WHY DOES SIMPLIFYING MATTER?

Society is being overwhelmed (and overrun) by transformative technological innovations that elude our capacity to monitor effects and consequences in anything but an "it's already too late to do anything about it" manner. Issues and urgencies that once were far away, remote, exotic, and foreign and — because of that — mostly ignorable, are now noisily and urgently camped on our doorstep. Do we feel as if we have any way to deal with those problems? Meanwhile, local issues and problems that once seemed relatively easy to fix go ignored or unaddressed. Every day, it's a new and seemingly impossible-to-solve crisis: roads, infrastructure, education, poverty and homelessness, inflation, wage and income inequities, international wars, terrorism, climate change, and so on, and it goes on and on. It all seems way too much for any one person to deal with. At the same time, we don't feel safe in our communities. Most of us feel more stressed out and less "in control."

It's no surprise that people are desperate for ways to simplify their lives.

WE'VE ALL SERIOUSLY TUNED OUT

Increased levels of disengagement, distraction, alienation — an attitude that "none of this matters" or that our problems are "too big" to solve so "what's the point?" and so on — are special challenges for the culture-driven leader. In other words, we aren't listening. Consider the following workplace statistics:[2]

- Just over half (53 percent) of employees agree that their boss values their opinion.
- As few as one-third (35 percent) feel inspired by their boss.
- One quarter believe they can do a better job than their boss.
- Almost 1 in 5 (17 percent) believe their boss takes credit for their work.
- Younger employees feel the least comfortable compared to older workers in challenging their boss's ideas.
- Only 35 percent of female employees feel comfortable challenging their boss's ideas.

"WE'LL BE FINE"

According to one study of the exploding mobile sector, 72 percent of customers will end up sharing a positive experience with six or more people. That sounds great, at first. What's interesting is that we might have assumed that unhappy customers are most likely to complain, but that turns out not to be true. In fact, only one of twenty-six customers on average will complain. The problem with that is that they are far more likely to spread news of their experience to others. You may not be hearing from your customers about poor or bad experiences, but chances are very high that customers are sharing their experiences with their friends and colleagues.

Listening to customers is vital. Responding to their comments and complaints is even more important. It turns out that when customers do take the time and trouble to complain, follow-up percentages are very low for most companies. That's taking a bad situation and making it worse. Criticism might not be great to hear, but leaders need to know what their customers — and employees — are saying. Not paying attention will likely result in disaster. It's the *Titanic*'s captain ignoring the news that the ship was about to hit an iceberg, saying, "We'll be fine."

Listening to customers is vital. Responding to their comments and complaints is even more important.

Outsourcing the task of customer feedback to a third party is a big mistake. It's not a data feed, it's the temperature gauge of your company's culture. If it's critical to the business, then it's best done in-house by committed people. Listening "creates" an "openness to failure" and a "willingness to experiment that sits at the heart"[3] of a successful company culture. A company like Virgin, for instance, is among the elite because of its focus on employee satisfaction and retention. Happy and enthusiastic employees — the ones who become valued ambassadors for the brand — embrace and embody the "value to the customer" mindset that underpins the "we will listen; we will simplify" commitment.

"I THOUGHT I WAS LISTENING!": A CASE STUDY FOR THE HARD-OF-HEARING CEO

It was one of the most popular and transformative brands the world has ever known: Starbucks. With more than thirty-eight thousand outlets around the world (there are more than sixteen thousand in the United States alone), Starbucks revolutionized the concept of drinking coffee. It also made a cultural hero of its founder, Howard Schultz, one of the most recognized and admired leaders in the world. He has been called "the good guy of American capitalism." He basically rewrote the conventional book on how to treat his employees by adopting a "we're all family here" approach that included health insurance, stock options, and other benefits unheard of at the time.

In 2021 the Starbucks story took a sharp turn — for the worse.* Employees began complaining about low pay, increased stress, and difficult working conditions. Pretty soon the complaints coalesced into a backlash that resulted in an unprecedented and unexpected decision: employees at 225 outlets voted to unionize. Schultz the "working class's hero" was being criticized as a "greedy" and "out of touch" billionaire.[4] Instead of dealing with his employees' grievances, Schultz was accused by one of the country's largest labour organizations of retaliatory tactics, including engineering a "virulent, widespread and well-orchestrated" campaign against his unionizing employees. He called the union mobilizers an "outside force that's trying desperately to disrupt our company."[5] The problem "wasn't that Starbucks was losing money or that demand" was "waning, but that corporate executives hadn't listened to their employees."[6] A Starbucks employee complained that they were "tired" of a CEO who sounded like "a disappointed father because they weren't grateful."[7]

Schultz eventually tried to make it right. "I need to hear everything, as much as you can share," he said at a meeting with employees in California.[8]

---

* By April 2023 the situation at Starbucks had not improved dramatically. In fact, by then Schultz had stepped down as CEO *for the third time*, having turned top leadership over to "outsider" Laxman Narasimhan. "One of the things we've talked about," the new CEO said of Schultz, "is that I may not always agree with him, and so we're going to privately obviously spend a lot of time talking about how we essentially come to a common point of view." If that objective sounds optimistic or even unrealistic, you'd be right: leaders need to lead. There can't be a committee at the top of the pyramid. (Noam Scheiber and Julie Creswell, "No Longer at Starbucks Helm, Howard Schultz Is the Focus at Labor Hearing," *New York Times*, March 28, 2023, nytimes.com/2023/03/28/business/starbucks-howard-schultz-senate.html)

A good lesson for any leader is being receptive to what needs to be heard, not what you want to hear. Now, not later.

LISTEN; SIMPLIFY: A HISTORY LESSON

At ING Direct, we needed to build a savings account that would make the sign-up process simple and easy, and save customers time and money, while encouraging a sustained savings behaviour.

In the traditional "onboarding" of customers, it usually takes on average about twenty minutes (or more) for the customer to complete a lengthy eleven-step legacy form. First question we asked: What is a customer's time worth to her or him? Not to us. Important! We didn't want to focus on what was less time-consuming for us, but for the prospective customer. Would they be happier and more enthusiastic filling out a shorter form? A form that was deliberately less repetitive? Why are you asking this? Why do I need to put this down a second time? Who thought this would take only twenty minutes?

We used two approaches. One was breaking out the first steps that had to be done to set up the account. Capture the basic facts. Name, address, email, phone number that a customer used in every retail transaction. Open the account and tell the customer it's open. We next identified the steps that needed to be taken to comply with regulatory rules when a first deposit was made. This was not visible to the customer. Last, we set out the remaining features. Automatic deposits, options to receive notifications or mail confirmations.

The idea was to break down the steps and shorten the time a customer had to spend setting the account up and starting. There was no need to do it all at once, and we could cut eleven steps to seven. We only collected data that was essential or required. It made the experience better, easier for the customer. It kept the value proposition alive in the customer's mind. It built trust and appreciation for respecting the customer's time.

It seems like almost every day we are faced with the mind-numbing, repetitive task of filling out forms; doctors, dentists, motor vehicle offices … We are asked to supply the same information, information that is already sitting in an electronic database. Why are we filling it all in again on paper for a frontline person to enter it again in a database? What amazes me on a daily basis is how many businesses make the same mistake over and over again: it doesn't matter what might end up being more convenient and cost-efficient to you and your business. What matters is what's convenient, what's easy for your customers.

First, you need to address the overall cost to the consumer of their time and effort; don't make assumptions about how you define a "simple process." It's not you filling out the forms! It's simple. In, fact, so simple that it's routinely ignored. Value your customer's experiences and expectations. If you don't, your business, no matter how great your product or service is, will be seen negatively.

Believe it or not, when we were about to launch ING Direct, I was thinking about my mother and her peers. I was worried her generation of consumers would be turned off or apprehensive about an online banking service. Would she (they) take to it? Would she (they) trust it? Would they ask too many questions?* What I hadn't asked at that point was the simplest and most direct questions of all: "Mom, what do you like about the way you currently do banking? What about not having a 'familiar face' at the counter? Would you be willing to consider an alternative?" I needn't have worried. "Yes," she said, "I'd absolutely try something different." She said her experience was fine overall, but most of the time, it was focused on driving to the bank, searching for parking, probably standing in line, seeing a new face behind the counter, that kind of thing. She was

> When we talk about principles like "we will listen" or "we will simplify" or "be fair," it is *always* directed at and defined by the *customer experience.*

---

* One of the most rewarding behaviours I adopted in my career is asking rather than presuming. It usually involved direct contact with customers. What do they want? It doesn't matter what we want. It's a low-tech approach, which is why it probably isn't that fashionable amongst many contemporary analytics-based executives. We collect and act on data; what we need is information — authentic and meaningful feedback. Customers will tell you what you need to know. Are you giving them a chance?

less concerned about the lower costs she would have doing online banking. What she (and her peers) valued more was the lower cost in terms of *her* time spent on services. So simple! And all I had to do was listen.

HEARING IS EASY; LISTENING IS HARD

A few years ago, I was invited to deliver a talk to a select group of professionals from the military. They were welcoming and gracious, even when I told them that my talk would focus on the value for any business or organization of creative destruction, meaningful transformation, small disruptive shifts versus large culture change, and how change can be implemented and sustained, where change can be found and nurtured, and so on — the nuts and bolts of my career as the banking industry's "rebel with a cause."

As the time for my speech approached, however, I sensed from the tight, nervous smiles I was seeing that it might be a good idea to scale back a bit on my emphasis on "disruption." The military, after all, is an organization culturally defined by traditions, rigid chain-of-command hierarchies, commitment to cause, duty, obedience, and loyalty. In this case, I decided that the group, while *theoretically* receptive and open to what I had to say, was not *genuinely* receptive as I had presumed.

Well, is that such a big deal? The answer is yes! Cultures are like people; we hear what we want to hear.

I have never delivered a message of any sort to any group (large or small) without having first taken "the temperature" of the room. It doesn't matter what I want to say. What are they going to hear? How do I align both?*

Are you tuned into the culture?

"YOU AREN'T LISTENING!"

We've all been in situations where a difficult conversation suddenly breaks off like two spent boxers in the ring. "Forget it. You aren't listening." Generally speaking, what the person is saying is, "You're not agreeing with me."

---

* For example, consider the communication fiasco that erupted during and after Elon Musk's high-profile takeover of X in 2023. It may have been a clever tactic on his part, of course.

It isn't easy for anyone in a leadership role to deal with criticism or disagreements. You will be faced with both, of course. It's inevitable. To minimize that, I have always found it worthwhile to solicit as much feedback as I can. First, it helps sharpen my awareness of what impact my decisions and judgments are having. Second, I often hear things that I would never hear and which I need to hear. Third, creating open communication channels helps create opportunities for increased investment from all levels in the outcome.

In practice, it's humbling. It's your customer who decides whether or not you meet the desire outcome. Everyone who works for you needs to be on board in order to make that happen.

A "listen and keep it simple" checklist

- Keep the focus on the customer experience.
- The basics for making something simple are to start with the user: what a user does; what a user needs. First, it should save time. To make something simple, make it intuitive. If you have to study it, learn, or guess your way to accomplishing a task, it's a product or service failure. If something needs a manual, there is basically a failure of design and delivery.
- Demand-side thinking is the rule for success. If you save time, effort, and energy to get something done, you will, in turn, save on costs and enhance efficiency. Make demand-side solutions first; look at the supply-side constraints and impacts second. It's the smart approach.
- Every 1-800 number (or any real-world equivalent) is a failure from a consumer-focused perspective. It doesn't matter how complicated or complex a product or service is "under the hood." From the consumer's perspective, it should be a very direct and simple A to B and done. If the consumer needs to call to have it explained, it's not simple. And you're not listening.

- Profile terrorism: demands for data and detail including but not limited to personal information are increasing at an alarming rate. Simple for the customer? No!
- What works best for you may not be what's best for your customer. Technology is not necessarily the answer all the time. Being on the wrong side of a computer-driven process can be expensive and disruptive.* AI may be a solution, for instance, but not the solution. Ask your customer what they want. More PINs? More passwords? More computer forms?
- Time is a resource; don't waste it. Not yours and especially not your customers'. Save me time first, then consider saving me money. The other way around is short-term thinking. Saving customers time will enable you to build their trust and confidence in the product, service, and business. The goal is to improve the customer's quality of life.

"I CAN'T HEAR MYSELF THINK!"

"When given the option of 'not buying,' it turns out that 'over-choice' — an overwhelming variety of options — actually turns customers or clients away. The analysis paralysis, anxiety, and panic that results from choosing between too many options is bad."[9]

We're all familiar with "preference paralysis." The problem of having to choose from so many options that we are overwhelmed and as a result are unable to decide. We are being yelled at and bombarded by too much *stuff*. If you are like me, you might see dozens of commercials a day about banks or cell phone plans offering services and plans. Very quickly, they all start to sound very much the same.

---

* Our almost childlike dependence on technology to solve our problems is not new, but neither is it the answer. Back in 1944, the poet T.S. Eliot warned about "the relentless pressure of modern industrialism." He worried that we had "become mechanized in mind, and consequently attempt to provide solutions in terms of engineering, for problems which are essentially problems of life." Isn't this what leadership provides? Human solutions to human problems?

For leadership, the problem is acute. We might not worry much about opting for one box of laundry detergent over another, but for a leader, the cost of choosing incorrectly can be hugely consequential. How many choices are ideal? One choice clearly is not ideal. It means we were trapped and our decision-making controlled. Two choices always create a kind of "door number one or door number two" tension: you are either right or wrong and the pressure of not being wrong — even more than the satisfaction of being right — is intense and can prove debilitating. Having three viable options tends to work best. It's classic and will prove a useful approach in the leadership toolbox.

> Culture-driven leadership comes to the rescue by creating a different approach to the customer and their experience.

Culture-driven leadership comes to the rescue by creating a different approach to the customer and their experience. In some cases it might be purely a question of dollars and cents: Which is cheaper? In other cases, it might have more to do with how your product or service meets customer preferences. It could be a million different scenarios. The point is that in general our executive-level thinking is often too disengaged with what is happening with the customer themselves. Simply, we aren't listening.

CONCLUDING THOUGHT

Listening to customers and simplifying services, and constantly revising how we are doing what we do, are cornerstones of culture-driven leadership. There is a very good reason why most of us don't believe the pitches we hear on TV. We don't feel we are being listened to, or that our concerns or preferences are being addressed. The more we hear that we matter, the less we believe it. And there is more and more of it every day. According to a recent survey, 60 percent of us feel "overwhelmed."[10] It's time for leadership to recognize and meet this challenge by reawakening our commitment to customer service and building a business culture that is committed to making delivery and service as creative and valuable as selling the product in the first place.

Listen! Simplify! Your customers win, and so will you.

ACTION POINTS

- Recognize that to simplify is very hard.
- Simplicity is how the customer or consumer rates (values) the experience.
- Listening is very difficult; most of us aren't very good at it. Distractions are everywhere and increasingly hard to avoid.
- Be open to what you need to hear, not what you want to hear. Knowing which is which is crucial.

Chapter 5

WE WILL BE FAIR

It's a judgment, but it's all encompassing. What is fair is always in the eye of the beholder. Being fair is the guiding light we follow in everything we do; it's a powerful tool to find and retain loyal customers and stakeholders. Your customers have options; give them reasons to choose you. Treat others the way you want to be treated. Imagine your mother walking through the door. What would she think of what you're doing? Would she approve? It seems so simple and a bit old-fashioned. Remember, your brand is what is said about you *behind your back*. What do you want to hear about you and your personal brand?

· · ·

In this chapter we'll be exploring the principle — and its unique challenges — that customers should be treated fairly. Not just customers, either, everyone. Unfortunately, of all the principles the idea that "we will be fair" is the most difficult to summarize. As we know, the word "fair" can be used in a number of different ways: treatment that is impartial and even-handed, for instance, is fair; work that is acceptable or adequate can be described as fair. Let's keep the first use in mind as we think about the overall retail landscape and what we as leaders ought to be doing, but too often are not. Truth is, "fair" can be harder to pin down in print than it is to see it in practice. What is fair can be aligned closely and even overlap with listening and telling the truth. In a company with a strong culture, it will be understood at all levels and function automatically. It will be the backdrop for every interaction and transaction.

We all have an instinct for what is fair. A child, for instance, will cry, "It's not fair," when they don't get what they want. The parent knows different; giving the child what they want simply because they want it would actually not be good for them. Most of us know what it's like to do our best (as conceived by us) and still end up on the wrong side of the stick. "Life's not fair."

What a customer wants and what your product or service provides is not always in perfect alignment. The media giant Netflix, for instance, recently started a tiered-payment system: those wanting commercial-free streaming are now required to pay an extra fee. Banking customers who keep a minimum cash balance (usually one that is very high and out of reach for most) in an account are treated better than those who don't. Certain fees are waived for them. It's standard practice to offer alluring perks to those who have larger bank balances. The point is, a customer may not want to pay extra for better service; however, the company may have good reasons for needing to raise fees. How does one satisfy two opposing requirements? Keeping the customer happy while hitting profit targets requires an incredibly tough and difficult balancing act. It is difficult for a leader to sustain that kind of balance. The idea behind the principle of "being fair" is preserving as much as possible the alignment between what a customer wants and what the customer gets.

> **What a customer wants and what your product or service provides is not always in perfect alignment.**

Here's the problem from my perspective. The streaming customers who decide that they don't mind paying a higher monthly fee for commercial-free viewing get what they want. For them, the higher cost is worth it. What about everyone else? What choice do they have? How exactly are their consumer preferences being met?

A huge part of being fair is focusing not on the customers whose preferences are being met but on the ones who are not. Not everyone is alike, so why do we treat them as if they are? We're not saying that there should not be luxury hotels or first-class airline service or platinum credit cards. What we are asking — or what we should be asking — is simple: What about everyone else? Aren't their needs and preferences worth addressing? Shouldn't they have a chance to invest in and benefit from the prosperity that more and more seems to be limited to an elite? As an entrepreneur with purely practical motives, why would you turn away from or look down on a potentially lucrative slice of the market? We didn't when we founded ING Direct. We made a conscious decision to focus on the needs of those not receiving the special perks from the mainstream banks. It worked!

Being fair means focusing not on the customers whose preferences are being met, but on everyone else.

Think of being fair as a covenant. We all know what a covenant is: an agreement between two parties for the performance of an action that is *mutually beneficial*. You do this for me, and I will do this for you. Unlike a contract, a covenant generally implies a much heavier obligation between the parties, and a heavier penalty for breaking its bonds. I have said many times that doing business is a privilege. I also think the relationships we as business leaders build with our customers should be treated as covenants.

It should be clear by now that the increasing complexity and the number of emergent disruptions faced by leaders today have pretty much upended a great deal of what we believed was conventional business practice and behaviour. If there are any leadership norms that remain from even a decade or so ago, I am not aware of them. It would be an exaggeration to say we are flying blind out there, but it's not really an exaggeration to say that it's dark and our depth perception is shot. Leaders who want to stick around and have a meaningful career need all the help they can get.

A good start might be getting back to the fundamentals and *keep getting back to them*. What do you do? How is it defined? What are its limitations and what are your core competencies and desired outcomes? Who are your customers? Is there maximum alignment? If so, you're being fair. It's when you find yourself having drifted off the main road that you'll know you're lost.

"DADDY'S BACK!"*

Let's consider an example that illustrates how important this principle is in practice. In late November 2022, Disney CEO Bob Chapek was fired. The move shocked the industry and generated enormous headlines (as well as incredible investor relief). Chapek was the hand-picked successor of former Disney CEO and legend Robert Iger. He had only recently had his contract renewed by the Disney board for an additional three years. What happened? Most of the reasons are what one might expect in a legendary fall from grace … except for one, which has not garnered as much attention as it might have: Chapek "disregarded" the Disney fans and they revolted.

According to a customer who self-identified as a Disney "super-fan" and "one of the many devoted Disney fans around the world," Chapek had been the target of a two-year super-fan-based campaign to have him ousted. Why? He "didn't believe in Disney magic." Disney, the super-fan stated, "is so much more than just another big business. Understanding that is crucial to its success. What Mr. Chapek doesn't understand, is the role we fans play in creating the Disney magic."[1]

This fan — and fans like him — wasn't getting what he wanted (and thought he deserved) from the new CEO. It clearly didn't matter whether or not the proposed changes would end up being good or bad for Disney's bottom line. Was his ouster from Disney fair? Bob Chapek probably wouldn't agree. What about the super-fans? The customer is always right, right?

---

* The nearly unanimous response of super-fans to the return of Robert Iger as CEO of Disney in November 2022.

Well, it's complicated. Short answer: no, not always.

The runway for leadership to get it all "right" gets shorter and shorter.*

It's possible that when tasked with the incredibly demanding challenges of running a huge and hugely complex global entertainment company — including navigating it through a worldwide pandemic — Chapek allowed himself to — if even temporarily and without intent — deprioritize the "customer experience." Unfortunately, in doing so he broke the bonds of the covenant, and there was no way back. Of Robert Iger's return, the super-fan Disney community was ecstatic. He "cared about our expectations, our level of satisfaction and our interests. What customers thought mattered."[2] Huge majorities of customers not only expect more from companies they deal with, they are not shy about making their disagreements and dissatisfactions known. No company today is immune to blowback.

> **The world is more complicated than it ever was; the timeframe for development is rapidly collapsing. Next week will be more complicated than last.**

Will it work? Will restoring Disney culture, for instance, be as simple as bringing back a beloved CEO? Maybe, but maybe not. "The world is a much more complicated place than it was a few years ago," a business insider reported at the time, "and it is going to be hard to live up to the reputation he built as the most formidable media CEO ever. And he's going to have a short runway to pleasing Wall Street, his staff, creative partners, and the audience."[3]

"So much for going out on top."†

---

* Hardly a day goes by without screaming headlines about another CEO being pushed onto the short plank. Bob Chapek was one. In early January 2023 — and after only ten months on the job — Southwest Airlines CEO Bob Jordan became another. And as we know, the future for Goldman Sachs CEO David Solomon suddenly has become rocky (see chapter 2).

† Iger's first act as the new CEO was to announce a plan to cut seven thousand employees in "a multibillion-dollar cost-cutting initiative aimed at streamlining the company's operations in a period of media industry turmoil." Not what workers at "the happiest place on Earth" wanted to hear but making difficult (and unpopular) choices is what CEOs are hired to do.

WHAT WOULD YOUR MOTHER THINK?

Let's consider another example of fairness in the marketplace. You sign up for a subscription to some product or service. Months later, you come across an email notification that the subscription has been automatically renewed. "I don't remember renewing," you think. And you're right. *You didn't.* The service provider decided for you. In other words, you had to "opt out" of a choice you hadn't realized you needed to make. It's not an accident; it's a feature that exists by design and is routinely employed to exploit the foibles of human psychology. Is taking advantage of a customer's enthusiasm (or inclination not to read the fine print) a fair business practice? Would you do the same thing to a friend or relative? If your mother found out, what would she think?

Another issue. Online privacy has become a huge concern for all of us, and rightfully so. Protecting it is becoming more and more of a problem, and it seems that big media isn't very interested in helping solve that problem. In May 2023, for instance, Google was forced to pay a $40 million penalty by a Washington state court to settle a lawsuit in which it was alleged that the company "gave consumers the false impression that they have more control over how the company collects and uses location data than they really do."[4] According to the suit, Google uses much of the data it harvests from its users for its large advertising business, which generated revenue of about $150 billion in 2020. That is a lot of incentive.

What about our privacy, however? Don't we have a right to keep what is ours? *It doesn't seem fair.*

Imagine a company showing up to install new locks on your house, and without your knowledge making duplicate keys and passing them around to whoever was willing to pay. We'd be outraged.

JUST SAY "NO"

When we built ING Direct, we eliminated the fine print. Customers who were thinking of signing up would know from the get-go exactly what was on offer. And we stuck to it. A huge challenge launching ING Direct was helping customers understand and come to terms with what exactly it was that set us apart from the competition; many were receptive, some were not, many had questions, and that was fine. If it's a hamburger you want, don't stop at the hot dog stand. If a customer balked at our conditions and terms, asked for exceptions, or demanded special treatment, we empowered our customer service team to say no. It's just not what we do. And they would be backed up all the way. Having and sustaining the buy-in from both sides (customers and employees) is what keeps the culture front and centre. It's how we defined "fair."

WHAT THIS MEANS IN PRACTICE

Being fair — especially in business — is extremely difficult. You have to always consider how what you do, how the decisions you make will affect others — customers, employees, shareholders, and so on. Doing that consistently over time is extremely hard. Life for a leader can get extremely hectic, and it's easy to lose focus and let priorities slip off the radar. "Being fair" doesn't mean making everyone happy; that's impossible. It means staying on course and allowing the power of your principles to lead and not be compromised.

How do you — as a leader — make that happen?

In the following examples I will take a sometimes direct but more

> **It isn't up to you to decide what's fair; your customer decides.**

often an indirect path to illustrate what "being fair" means in practice and how culture-driven leadership keeps you on track. The examples will range far and wide. This is important because the challenges leaders are facing today and tomorrow will be virtually unlimited in number and will come from unexpected directions. Response times, as we know, which once might have been generous and afforded time for reflection and planning, have shrunk, making it more important than ever that we get it right the first time. There will not be a second time.

Remember that "being fair" means being true to your principles and ruthlessly consistent in how they are interpreted and applied. If that means you need to drop or "fire" a customer who wants special treatment, do it. Being fair means sustaining and reinforcing the alignment between customer and product or service.

LIFE IS LIKE A BLACKBOARD THAT CAN'T BE ERASED

I said fairness was hard to define. It is, and the problem only gets worse when thinking about the many different situations a leader faces in any given day. What follows are examples of fairness in practice that I've culled from my own career both as a CEO and a keen observer of business and leadership over the years. It's not being fair, but the realities of leadership can challenge and undermine a culture where fairness is a foundational pillar of company behaviour.

I said above the customer tends to decide what is fair, but customers aren't the only ones who want a say in deciding what's fair.

A huge evolution in management-employee relations has taken place. The traditional "9 to 5, I do what the boss tells me to do" mindset has been replaced by a worker-centric "I am here to be fulfilled" perspective. It's more complicated than that, of course, but workplace relationships are increasingly focused on individual satisfaction. Customers aren't the only ones that need attention. Employees demand that too. The same questions you ask about your customer need to be asked of the people who have chosen to sign on with you. It's not work anymore; it's a journey. A culture-driven leader needs to understand our new landscape and how to balance expectations with the need for a desired outcome. Moving too much in one direction or the other undermines alignment and threatens outcomes. It's important to remember that being fair won't always result in being popular or well-liked. A parent's or teacher's job is hard because they're required to do what is best for the child

> **Employees evaluate a leader and decide if they are worthy of respect, if they can be trusted, based on many things.**

We Will Be Fair

or student, even when that's not what the child or student wants. And in business, you're dealing with adults who have a fully developed sense of who they are and what they want, of what they are willing or not willing to do. Creating and sustaining alignments in this individualistic ecology — in other words, being fair — is a challenge.

How to start? As a leader, you need to establish boundaries. Employees evaluate a leader and decide if they are worthy of respect, if they can be trusted, based on many things. What impression do you want to make? Whatever that is, it needs to be consistent. That doesn't mean just being consistent in what you say and do in your professional life. There are no guardrails anymore that clearly separate a person's private life from their professional one. For leaders today, there is no "off the record" behaviour. Everything counts. And everything is being counted. I used to tell young managers, "Be careful with the water cooler talk." Be aware of your demeanour and behaviour at all times. Know where you are and what is expected or anticipated. Truth is, by taking on a leadership role, you voluntarily take on burdens, responsibilities, and obligations that others don't. It's the personal cost of leadership. If you are not respected, your decisions will be questioned and challenged. Look at Howard Schultz. He assumed his employees were happy; they resented him, complained, and rebelled.

Being fair means it all counts and cannot be erased. If you think life's like a blackboard that you can erase and do over, you can't.

IF YOU WANT A RELATIONSHIP, GET A DOG

Leadership can be a lonely existence. A leader needs to be respected and that requires maintaining a prescribed distance. In a business environment, decisions that are critical to outcomes need to be made and (most important) accepted and understood. It's an issue I have with the many tech startups, for instance, that thrive on a "let's party" atmosphere that can blur the decision-making hierarchies. Being fair requires consistent leadership, which often requires making difficult or unappealing decisions.

A leader has to know the role they are playing 24-7. You can't hide or break out of character to "hang out with the guys." I was at a year-end celebration in New York and was invited to join the troops for a drink. It sounded like a great idea, and a perfect opportunity to mingle in a less formal environment where we could all relax. About an hour later, I was eased aside. "What's up?" I asked. It was suggested I might want to leave the party. "Why? What's wrong?" Nothing, I was told. "It's just that ..."

It was a eureka moment for me about the "always on" role of leader, and especially about who we want leaders to be — what we need leaders to be. My employees had their friends and colleagues, their office mates and acquaintances, and then there was me. Bottom line: we all have roles to play, and our behaviour needs to adjust and adapt to the role. Your obligation as a leader is to know who you need to be in order to get the job done. Who your employees need you to be, who your customers need you to be. You need to be that thing. Remember: it's not about you; it's about the outcomes.

It also helps to have a bit of mystery about you, as well!

IF IT WERE ONLY THAT EASY!

A traditional game for young children is "follow the leader." The rules are (or seem to be) quite simple. One child is chosen leader, and all the other kids are obliged to copy every movement the leader makes. Whoever doesn't is out. The child who remains at the end of the game is declared the winner and becomes the leader for the next round.

If it were only that easy. Psychologists tell us that games like this (there are thousands) are instrumental when it comes to how we learn important and useful skills for life as adults. The most important lesson from the game, of course, is learning how to *follow instructions.* Doing that will sometimes require doing things you don't like doing or doing things that you don't agree with. I have had to do things that I wasn't particularly interested in doing, but, nevertheless, I was judged on and evaluated on my performance of those tasks. That's just the way it is.

That being said, it's important that what's being asked is fair — not just in a general way but also particularly. That means that it should be fair to expect the individual asked to perform what's being asked. It's not fair to expect more than what's possible. Instructions need to be fair. Sometimes training is needed. Sometimes more resources are needed. Sometimes deadlines need to be altered. However, sometimes that's not possible. Sometimes an employee just isn't a good fit. It's unfortunate that perfectly nice and enthusiastic people are sometimes not the right fit for a job, that they can't do what needs to be done. It happens. Outcomes need to be met. What's important is that expectations are clearly communicated. If they aren't, employees will feel that they haven't been treated fairly. And they'll be right.

Communication isn't easy, though. It is harder these days for leaders to be heard. There are celebrity leaders like Elon Musk who seem to be in the headlines every day, sharing their opinions about this or that, but that is not what I mean. Being "heard" requires communicating a message that will be considered, will be understood. If what is be-

> **It's important that what's being asked is fair.**

ing communicated is fair, it will be embraced, not only by the customer but by everyone with whom you work. A leader needs to be respected; it's just as important that everyone is willing to follow the leader. Are they willing to follow you? We talked earlier about fairness being a covenant. I do what I promise, and you do what you promise in return. A culture-driven leader needs not only to lead but to create an environment where everyone is invested in the outcomes.

It's your responsibility to create that culture and to make sure it is sustained.

I have had many opportunities both in my corporate career and my time as a professor to quiz students about their leadership ambitions. I like to ask a prospective leader the following question: "Why should I follow you?"

It's a basic issue of fairness.

THE CARROT OR THE STICK?

Leaders are commonly faced with the problem of what to do when an employee underperforms or fails to meet expectations. As noted earlier, the key to resolving performance problems is having the discipline and awareness to adapt different styles of leadership to the situation. That's not as simple or straightforward as it might seem. First, you need to determine if you have correctly read the situation. Perhaps the instructions were not clear, or the individual was not allowed a chance to have it made clear? Then there's the question of whether or not they have the requisite skill set required for completing the task. How was the outcome defined? Was the time-frame adequate?

Generally speaking, an individual is either capable of completing a task but doesn't (a potential "stick" scenario), or they aren't capable and so don't have the capacity to complete the task (a "carrot" scenario). Sounds simple enough, but as Mies van der Rohe, the famous architect, said, God is in the details, and knowing how to employ a carrot or a stick to drive the culture is an art form.

To resolve the problem, I have to remember what my role is, number one. And number two, what the other person understands my role to be. Third, I need to be clear about what it is I need to get done.* Will I get the best result by being supportive, understanding, and constructive? Or would it be better to honestly critique, demand changes, and push back for more effort and improvement? Whichever approach is taken, it's essential to deal with the situation in a manner that is consistently and irreproachably professional.

> **It's your responsibility to create the right culture and to make sure it is sustained.**

The task is made easier if the right culture is in place and driving performance metrics. If everyone understands the mission and their role in the outcome, has the support, opportunities, and resources necessary to achieve the outcome, performance (or lack thereof) can be measured objectively. The sign of a deteriorating culture is performance decisions or criteria that are inconsistent or subjective.

---

* It's another fascinating reason to look deeper into the decisions being made by Elon Musk. What exactly is it that he is trying to get done with so many of his unorthodox leadership decisions? Do employees flourish in an environment where the outcomes are not clearly defined and consistent?

HERDING CATS

A good leader needs to balance the need to allow their employees space to do their jobs with the need to keep a clear eye on performance and outcomes. Allowing the reins to be loose can lead to confusion; keeping them too tight can lead to frustration. A culture-driven leader needs to tolerate a certain amount of chaos and accept that not all things will be perfect. It's very common for leaders to adopt a restrictive leadership style ("This is the way it's done"). It's a control issue.

Bottom line: take a step back; it's cats.

THE HUGE COST OF CULTURAL DISSONANCE

It's hard to maximize customer satisfaction if employee buy-in and trust are not fostered. Concepts like "trust" and "fairness" can't be just empty slogans. Companies need to demonstrate their commitment to them — with their customers and with their employees. A leader is both the source and the primary custodian of culture; it is up to them to ensure that that commitment is kept. In May 2022, employees at SpaceX, the aeronautics company founded by Elon Musk, wrote an open letter criticizing the CEO for what they considered his unusual and erratic behaviour. "It is critical to make clear to our teams and to our potential talent pool that his messaging does not reflect our work, our mission, or our values."[5]

Musk "promptly fired several of them, claiming the letter was distracting the company from its mission (which is, of course, exactly what the letter claims Mr. Musk was doing)."[6] According to one critic, Musk represents the "kind of leader" who "believes he is the biggest asset to the company, so his interests are naturally paramount and his right to do and say whatever he wants should be unconstrained, with no regard to consequences."

FAIRNESS IS ABOUT ACCOUNTABILITY

Someone must be held accountable for a company's performance and actions to its stakeholders. The leader or CEO is the natural choice. Everyone is happy to join in success and share the fruits that come with the outcome.

And that is as it should be. On the other hand, not many people want to be associated with failure; nor do they want to be held accountable for it. And that, too, is as it should be. Your role as a leader is not to take credit for success but to be the first to step up and take the blame for failure. Missed outcomes, after all, are your failure. Ultimately, no one cares why something fails.

IS EVERYONE ON BOARD WITH YOUR CULTURE?

The hardest part of ensuring a business stays on course (respects its culture) is keeping the focus on the customer and the customer experience. I said earlier that employee buy-in has to be substantial. The team has to feel the same way about the importance of customer experience. One of the best moves I ever made was fully empowering our team members to make important customer decisions. They also had annual opportunities to vote me out of my job!* As a leader, you need to keep getting your team to buy in. Don't expect them to just sign up and leave it at that. Buy-in needs to be constantly refreshed. Team building — having a chain of command that communicates well — is the most important challenge for any leader; having to make the difficult decisions and choices and still keeping everyone onside and moving forward is extremely difficult.

TO BE A GOOD LEADER, FIRST BE A GOOD FOLLOWER

I credit 80 percent of my success to having hired the right people. This surprises people when I tell them, but it shouldn't. A leader obviously has a huge role to play, but it isn't any bigger or more critical than having the right people in place to carry out and implement the strategies. A conductor has a special skill set; ultimately, it's the quality of the orchestra that counts.

You may be thinking that you might make a good leader one day. I hope so. Here's a question: Do you know what it takes to be a good follower? I

---

* The trouble Howard Schultz is having with his Starbucks franchises (discussed earlier) is an excellent illustration of how buy-in (employee buy-in in this case) can deteriorate over time or with changes of context (or both).

don't think a person can be a good leader until they have been a good follower. (Think of the "follow the leader" example from earlier.) To be a good follower requires discipline and being objective in carrying out duties and assignments and taking an active part in the mission. It's a job, a role, and the duties and tasks are important to achieve the right outcome.

I think we have all experienced the "start from the bottom" work situation. Learn the job, become an expert about the product or the service. Following is not easy. It involves a learning curve (often a quite steep one). Always. How you get through it is key. If you are a good listener and focused on the task, willing to learn and apply yourself, progress can be made and goals met.

Following, however, is difficult. I've been there, and it can be very frustrating, especially if you are energetic, anxious, and bursting with ideas. Yes, keeping your ego in check is fundamental. Improving your skill set is the objective. Knowing how everything is meant to work — what that means and what is required — can be learned by having done it. You may have your own ideas, but unless and until you have learned how to take direction and prove you know how to *drive outcomes*, you'll be far less capable of confidently giving direction. It requires that you be open and receptive.

> **Keeping your ego in check is fundamental.**

Do I understand the outcome? Do I know how my contribution will be judged or graded? Stick to the script. Know what you are being asked to do from the front and back end. And remember that you are part of a team. Your success means little if it comes at a cost to others. The goal will only be reached as a result of the sum of all efforts. In other words, be humble. Nothing impresses a boss more than a team member who effectively and efficiently drives outcomes. Save the drama for community theater.

In evaluating candidates for leadership, it's a good idea to check what kind of a follower the candidate was. An example: I remember a candidate for a senior position at ING Direct. He had the just the right "professional banker" look: conservative but stylish suit, personable and well-mannered; his resumé was impressive, his experience more than adequate, and so on.

I made a note, however, that on a tour of the offices he was very respectful to senior people he met but ignored junior people: what's known as "kiss up and ignore down." I knew right away that he would not be the best person when it came to the leadership skills necessary to manage people effectively. The larger the leadership responsibilities, the less the resumé matters; it's more about character.

Character is the X factor in leadership.

NO ONE CAN DO IT ALONE

Even Jesus needed twelve disciples. I joke with friends about what would have happened if Jesus had had an HR department that did his disciple candidate screening. The point is, finding a quality team is about character and needs to be taken beyond the limited utility of a resumé.[*]

I had a number of techniques — parlor tricks — that I used. For instance, I asked the person if they minded if I read their palms. The reactions were always different. I'm not a professional palm reader, of course, but I did learn the basics from my grandmother and had a knack for it. The exercise wasn't the point. It was a way I could study a person under unusual or unexpected circumstances. How did they react? Were they open, receptive, and intrigued? Or did they shy away, close up, and withdraw? It's surprising how reliable the trick was. The point was to learn as much as possible in an interview to, hopefully, make better judgments.

It wasn't perfect, of course. Sometimes a hire just didn't work out. And sometimes a good hire stopped performing well. Being fair can mean admitting that an employee or team member has stopped "buying in" or has become a source of disruption. The fair (but very hard) decision is to admit your mistake. Yes, *your* mistake. A bad hire is a failure in leadership. Own it. And act quickly. Remember, it's the culture that matters. If it stops working, nothing you can do will save it.

------

[*] A regrettable consequence of the digital revolution, in my experience, has been exaggerating the utility of the resumé. Yes, skills are important. But *character is decisive*. People are not dollar-a-dozen hammers that can be shuffled around or easily replaced. Remember the "well-invested" promise from chapter 3? *If you live the values, join us on our journey. You won't regret it.* The thousands of people who were laid off in March 2023 by the Silicon Valley tech industry were not just resumés; they were people.

Buy in is so important, in fact, when I was CEO at ING Direct, I asked the staff to vote if they wanted me to lead another year. A cheap stunt? Not at all. Usually, the board of directors and shareholders are the ones to decide the fate of a CEO. I figured, why the board of directors? Yes, they represent the shareholders, but they focus on results and can't judge the process or the sustainability of the company. Are they in a better position to judge my performance than the people who actually show up every day and see me doing my job? To be honest, having the vote of confidence from employees mattered far more to me than the formal approval of the board. Action speaks louder than words.

I am still very proud of the fact that many of the workplace innovations we introduced caught on with leaders in other businesses. Some are now TV reality shows today! The riskiest workplace innovation we introduced — many at the time said it was the most foolish and reckless — was creating a "CEO for the Day" program: a job switch where I did someone else's job, and they did mine. After all, if it was important for me and our managers to know what life was like on the front lines, why not the reverse? Wouldn't it help reinforce trust to introduce "the front line" to what life was like at my end? I can't tell you how many times I have been in jobs where I overheard disgruntled employees grousing about how easy management had it. Well, did we? Do we? Why not try it for a day?

A bad hire is a failure in leadership. Own it.

Of course, we had to observe a few obvious ground rules. But that wasn't really the point. It was a magnificent opportunity to test how work gets done by watching how others think work should get done. And here is the most memorable lesson for me: they generally did my job much better than I did theirs! Talk about a humbling, grounding experience. I'll never forget it.

CONCLUDING THOUGHT

Yes, a leader should have compassion. The goal is always to bring the team member onside. But at what cost? A leader must temper compassion with the discipline (and humility) required to make the hard choices.

Be fair to your employees. Be fair to your customers.

You won't regret it.

ACTION POINTS

- "Being fair" is a compass direction in everything we do; it's a powerful tool to create loyal customers and stakeholders. Treat others the way you want to be treated. Seems simple, but it is often overlooked.
- If you're wondering and in doubt, just ask yourself what your mother would think. She'll set you straight!
- Start early! Before doing anything else, get exposure to as many circumstances as possible. Understanding oneself and seeing others in objective ways is not easy and not everyone is cut out for leading; if you are, be purposeful and take action.
- Before you can lead, you should know how to follow.
- Culture is the set of behaviours, values, and principles that dictate our actions individually and collectively. Leadership is the basis for how we get it done. Principles like "we are new here" and "we will be fair" keep leadership grounded. Stay on track.

Chapter 6

WE WILL TELL THE TRUTH

Too often, important information is left out or de-emphasized when consumers are offered products or services to choose between. Telling only the partial truth — or adopting strategies that encourage consumers to make false assumptions based on limited information — creates a lot of friction and delays. If consumers are not given the "whole story," if they are forced to ask too many questions to get the whole story, the frustration of not getting complete answers, of getting the run around, will damage the relationship and the company's reputation. If they are not given all the facts, or are not being listened to, the result will be too much space for misunderstanding. To tell the truth is to be upfront, direct, consistent, complete, and transparent. Importantly, the consumer has to be given and has to understand the whole story. The consumer doesn't have to agree with what they are told; they only have to accept it.* The truth has to be heard and understood.

Truthfulness requires the capacity for being aware and for being responsible. It requires being accountable to others and to yourself.

---

* Remember Jack Nicholson's brutal "You can't handle the truth!" comeback in the movie *A Few Good Men*? He played an honourable Marine Corps commander accused of dishonourable acts. His defence is a familiar one: we (the civilians) want our safety, security, and prosperity but don't want the gory details. The point for us in our discussion is who decides? The consumer? Or you?

. . .

For years, no American child could escape elementary school without learning the inspiring story of the six-year-old George Washington and the cherry tree. Asked by his father if he had chopped down the tree with his new hatchet, George admitted that he had. "I cannot tell a lie." That the incident never occurred is beside the point; the story is told to reinforce one of the important social and cultural norms that make society work, i.e., you should always tell the truth.

Rituals and ceremonies are engaged in for the same reason. A Las Vegas wedding officiated by an Elvis impersonator is just as legally binding as a big formal wedding in a church (or synagogue or mosque or temple) surrounded by family and friends. But which *means* more? Religion and the military used to provide the most familiar ceremonies and ritual-based activities, but fewer and fewer people today participate in those. And the traditions that people used to share in their personal lives are less frequently observed — even the once-a-week family dinner has become a rarity. It seems like most of us have retreated into increasingly private worlds where ritual and ceremony have mostly disappeared.

The problem with this, of course, is that — as with so many things that really matter — we don't realize how much we are losing until it's too late.[*] It's through rituals and ceremonies that we find out and reinforce what's important. And that generally involves something larger and greater than us.

So, what does this have to with "truth" and culture-driven leadership?

What makes culture-driven leadership so challenging is that we have less and less in common. Differences seem to matter more than any similarities that we share. Even truth has lost its authority. We talk about "truthiness" or "my truth," and we're not sure what that means.[†] How can we hope to create trust with our customers in this kind of environment? For a business leader today, trust is very

---

[*] The Covid-19 pandemic, ironically, taught us how important our rituals are by completing shutting down all social activity. The prom, high school graduations, sporting events, birthdays and weddings, retirement parties, and so on.

[†] According to recent surveys, 85 percent of fifteen-year-olds could not "reliably distinguish fact from fiction in reading tasks." Meanwhile, "more than half of U.S. adults had trouble identifying fact from fiction after reading a list of ten statements." (Stephen Johnson, "86% of American 15-year-olds can't distinguish fact from opinion. Can you?" Big Think, December 9, 2019, bigthink.com/the-present/opinions-facts/)

hard to establish and even harder to sustain. What I am suggesting and what I hope this chapter will show is the power of culture-driven leadership to create value and meaning via the concept of truth. Trust and truth are inseparable.

WE CAN'T EMBRACE WHAT WE DON'T TRUST

An example from late October 2022 illustrates what I mean. Just hours after Elon Musk finalized his takeover of the social media platform X, he created controversy by appearing to reverse course on promises he'd made to employees about mass layoffs *and* by posting a link to a "factually challenged" news report he later removed.* As one industry pundit noted, Musk's decision-making style represented "a complicated path ahead, particularly in navigating" his "public actions and squaring that with what he says privately."[1] "Elon Musk," added another, "has embraced managerial incompetence as if it were an emerging art form that requires great creativity."[2]

Among his first leadership actions was requiring employees to sign pledges commanding "hardcore" commitments (including extra hours and sleeping at the office). How far does personal commitment go?

And what about trust? Will X employees look back fondly at their tenure with pride and a sense of real fulfillment?

WHAT IS THE TRUTH?

We should expect the truth from leaders, and the consequences for leaders of failing to deliver that ought to be significant. What used to be called "shame" was a common form of social corrective. Today, we shame the

---

* A leader's behaviour cannot be separated from the brand. In this case, messaging matters. Musk, for instance, may have had excellent reasons for wanting to dramatically shake up the culture at X. The problem was not with the ends, but the means. It's hard to identify the A to B in his behaviour. It's hard to see how the short-term disruption (CEO-driven "my way or the highway" tactics) he caused would serve the long-term ambitions (a healthier culture and more productive company). If the goal, for instance, was to create a platform that put the "free" back into free speech, he could simply have asked for a show of hands. "Who believes we serve a higher cause?" A culture-driven leader creates opportunities for alignment, not occasions for division. Not only did he not do that, he actually damaged the viability of X. To correct things, Musk was forced to re-hire many employees he had fired; he came to realize that he didn't have a good understanding of how X actually worked.

shamers. An obvious problem for most of us in the social media age is that we are being exposed to so many spurious and suspicious claims and dubious or flat-out false statements that we can't seem to trust anyone or believe anything. Does that mean the truth doesn't exist?

Take a step back and think about the products and services you are happy with versus those that you aren't. What were you told about them? How did that product or service match the pitch? Where did the claim hold up and where might it have fallen short? If the product is a box of laundry detergent or a frozen pizza, it might be easy to decide. But what about a new app or smart device? How do you decide what works and what doesn't? Well, at one time, being an informed consumer might have been easy enough, but today, when so much of our world comprises of advanced technology that surpasses our ability to understand, it's frequently impossible to be properly informed about what we buy. Caveat emptor — buyer beware — is the rule, but more often than not these days, we aren't even sure what we need to beware of. It isn't a question of trust, but of blind faith.

WHAT YOUR CUSTOMER DOESN'T KNOW HURTS YOU

A pair of Apple AirPods wireless headphones retail for about $200. It's an amazing piece of state-of-the-art technology. The thing is, they only work for a year or so — usually less than a year. Then the battery runs out. This wouldn't be a problem *if it were it possible to replace the batteries.* Unfortunately, the batteries are fixed permanently into the unit. The devices, one online source states, "are designed so that the battery is not user-replaceable." It's a frustrating and costly extra charge that is *not publicized* anywhere in the product's promotional material.*

---

* Reality check: if companies always told the unvarnished truth, innovation would collapse; nothing comes to market as a perfect product. There are fans of innovative media technology who are happy to splurge on the newest wireless headphones, even if they will need to replace them when the battery runs out, because they want the newest and best. We need pioneers on both sides of the fence: innovators and the consumers willing to support the innovation. However, if a company is going to advertise that it is producing a "better product," it should be consistently committed to building a product that is as good as it can be. Could AirPods be equipped with replaceable batteries? Perhaps not. That's fine. If the technology exists, however, and it has simply been ignored in order to promote sales, it will be hard for consumers to trust the company.

Should we be wondering if the average customer is okay with the idea of investing $200 on equipment they might need to replace in twelve months? Failing to disclose, up front, information that might change the decisions a customer makes is not telling the truth.

A technology writer asked, "Should the customer be okay with a this-is-just-how-technology-works assumption?" No, he suggested, because the reality is "that's just how tech companies make more money from you."[3] The built-for-obsolescence manufacturing approach that started in the 1950s and made popular a just-throw-it-away attitude is still very much alive today. When was the last time you heard someone ask, "How long will this last?"* If we really wanted to help the environment, we could start by enforcing "built-to-last" initiatives. Doing that would go a long way to helping companies solve trust issues, as well.

For the culture-driven leader, it comes down the simple basics: Do right by the customer. Treat others how you wish to be treated. Would your mother approve? If you have doubts or aren't sure or think she probably wouldn't approve, you may want to reconsider your actions. When you (as leader) commit to valuing the customer and the customer experience, employees will see this attitude as having value; it helps boost morale and a sense of shared

Do right by the customer.

identity and purpose. When embraced and made tangible by action, the principle "we will tell the truth" becomes the ceremony by which value is celebrated and reinforced. If customers *perceive* that a company is being truthful — that it delivers what it promises — trust will be created, and they will be loyal to the brand. We all want to be valued for what we do. When customers tell us we're doing a great job, it matters.

---

* Americans throw away more than 420,000 cell phones every day; 151.8 million phones trashed in a single year. (Charmaine Crutchfield, "Smartphone disposal poses security risk, experts say," *USA Today*, November 10, 2014, usatoday.com/story/news/nation/2014/11/10smart-phone-security-risks/18798709/)

TRUTH CAN EASILY GET LOST

I was involved in the launch of a U.S.-based banking company. The company fell under the regulatory jurisdiction of both the Federal Deposit Insurance Corporation (FDIC) and the SEC's Options Clearing Corporation (OCC), which meant that we had to spend thousands of hours huddling with dozens of lawyers over months and months to deal with the mind-bogglingly complex banking-regulation hurdles. What unexpectedly proved even more daunting was attempting to answer all the questions and concerns potential customers expressed in the many focus groups we organized to test product value. The banking regulators' requirements we expected, and there were very few surprises; often, the questions customers asked were completely unexpected. What they wondered about was often unpredictable.

"Well," I said at the time, "based on all this feedback, if we're going to really explain how this is going to work, we'll have to really expand our product description."

I didn't expect this to be a controversial suggestion. Immediately, however, the legal team balked. Essentially, legal worried that if we did anything more than meet the banking requirements as outlined by the FDIC and OCC, we would be "opening the company up to liabilities" and who knows what additional expenses if the product did "not work out as a customer might expect."

I understood their concerns, but I countered that our responsibility as a company with a new product was to make sure it worked as a customer might expect. Our obligation was to make sure we were upfront about what it was, how it worked, and what to expect. Bottom line: the product description that the world of legal requirements and regulations produced, dozens of column inches of fine print, didn't correspond to the "plain English" truth of what the product was and what a customer could *believe* it could do.

It was an eye-opening moment. Our legal team had a "they can't handle the truth" opinion of our customers and the text they wanted reflected that. And they had a point! There was no easy way to explain every possibility or outcome, right? Is it *ever* possible to make a product or service foolproof? Can every possible situation related to the use of a product or service be presented in the description? If not, where is the line drawn? A complicating factor was that we couldn't possibly afford to create international support outlets everywhere they might be needed. Depending on or relying on the good will and understanding of customers was unstable. We needed to get it right and — ideally — right out of the gate. We created Q&A explanations that were as comprehensive as we could make them, but was that enough?* Data suggests that customers tend not to read disclaimers. The product had to be stable and work well without support. Every call would in effect be a system failure.

We chose to inform customers that the product might have certain issues (we listed them) under a variety of identified circumstances. We provided work-around options in advance and explained why there were limitations. Happily, the advance-warning effort was well accepted. The feedback was fantastic, in fact. In this case, being upfront — taking the time and effort to be as transparent as possible — proved absolutely critical to overcoming uncertainty and resistance for customer acceptance. Was it perfect? No, it wasn't. Our goal at that debut stage was not perfection but *satisfaction*. First, did the product do as much as the customer needed it to do? And what they expected it to do? Second, did it create *perceived value* for the customer? It did. We celebrated — briefly — then immediately began the process of making it better.

> **The *whole* story: If you think you are explaining to a customer all they need to know, how do you explain the "small print"?**

"Beta testing" is commonplace these days, of course. Especially in the technology-based sectors, it's a cost-conscious and time-saving method for identifying flaws and vulnerabilities. That's a good thing. We would all be better off with a lot more testing. There is a problem, though, with the comprehensiveness of the testing. Shortcuts may have been taken if market-delivery times were threatened. This kind of behaviour is common when tech products, especially software, are launched.

---

* Shampoo bottles still come with printed instructions, which seems absurd. Is it? Think about what might be going on there.

A landmark report from the U.S. government's Department of Homeland Security stated that "90 percent of security incidents ... result from exploits against defects in software."[4] A 2020 study from Positive Technologies claimed that "84 percent of companies have high-risk vulnerabilities on their external networks." More than half of those vulnerabilities, the study claimed, "could be removed simply by installing updates."[5] In 2021 the Cybersecurity and Infrastructure Security Agency — the nation's top cybersecurity agency — issued a warning "that a new, easy-to-exploit software vulnerability has likely led to hundreds of millions of computer hacks around the world."[6]

From where I sit, it seems a fair question to simply ask, "How responsible am I expected to be when it comes to protecting myself and my business from flaws and vulnerabilities in the products I (and billions of their customers) are using every day?" It's like my bank asking me to show up every night to make sure the door to the safe where I have my life savings deposited is closed and secured. Isn't protecting my money *their* job? Aren't we as leaders supposed to make customers *more* rather than *less* confident and trusting of the services and products we provide? In strong culture-driven leadership, truth is a commitment to the mission that is understood and shared by everyone: what is true for the highest individual in the company hierarchy is equally true for the lowest member. No exceptions. The same is true for the customer.

DO WE HAVE TRUST ISSUES?

In a recent survey that should scare the pants off any business leader, 81 percent of consumers insisted that "trust is a deciding factor in purchase decisions." However, only 34 percent of consumers "had trust in the brands they used."[7]

It isn't just consumers who have issues with trust. According to a recent "State of the Global Workplace" Gallup survey, only 33 percent of employees "strongly agree" with the statement that the company they work for "would never lie to our customers or conceal information that is relevant to them." In another survey, less than half of employees (46 percent) placed "a great deal of trust" in their employers.[8] In fact, globally, a whopping 74 percent of employees believe corruption "is widespread among businesses." Closer to home, only 23 percent of employees surveyed in a 2021 Gallup survey "strongly agree" that they "trust the leadership of their organization."[9]

Those numbers are worrisome. We need to do a lot better. We need to take a deep dive into how we are doing things and ask ourselves why we are doing it so poorly. Not tomorrow or the next day. Today. Right now.

Trust is earned over time; it requires long-term commitment to truthful practices. Where the rubber meets the road. It isn't always easy to tell the truth; in my experience; however, it's even harder not to tell the truth. And the consequences are much worse. And leaders have the biggest role to play in telling the truth.

You may think, for instance, that most people quit their jobs because they are unhappy with the salary. Not true. Most employees (75 percent) leave their jobs because they are unhappy with or have lost confidence in their boss. Interestingly, 63 percent of employees who are satisfied with their jobs state that the reason is that their employer treats them with respect. In fact, it should come as absolutely no surprise by now that a huge percentage of workers (79 percent) believe "company culture" is an important factor in overall job satisfaction.[10]

> **Trust is earned over time; it requires long-term commitment to truthful practices.**

It follows that creating a company culture built on truth (trust) should be of ultimate concern to any leader who hopes to succeed running a business. It's about respect. When you tell your customers and your employees the truth, you earn their respect. When someone says, "I really like my boss" what they really mean is, "I am being allowed to do what I really want to do, and I am really proud to be here."

The same is true for customers. Respect ensures that they will feel good about the decisions they have made. Remember, I told customers up front that it didn't matter how much money they deposited with ING

Direct, that the interest rate would be the same. True, a small number of people went elsewhere. They weren't angry; it just wasn't for them. In fact, even customers who ended up not banking with us generally had positive feelings about the overall value of what we were trying to do: innovating in the banking system.

When your company mission statement and the product or service descriptions have no hidden agenda and no small print — they are fully transparent — a customer has no need to read between the lines. The simple truth becomes your most powerful and reliable asset. Your customers will love it, and your employees will feel empowered and more likely to work harder as positive and enthusiastic ambassadors of the brand.

But let me warn you, telling the truth is easy … *at first*. What's really hard is telling the *same* truth over time (in other words, across changes of context). Leadership, of course, to be successful needs to remain flexible and always be attentive to what's coming down the road. A leader needs to pay attention to the moment, but they also have to plan for the future. Telling the truth is a powerful and difficult tool in that effort.

Today the buzz is "innovation." It doesn't seem to matter what business you're in — it must be innovative. It might be the right approach; it might be the wrong approach; what's key is that it be branded the innovative approach. That it sound high-tech and state-of-the-art, even (especially) when it isn't. The CEO of the sandwich chain Subway justified a recent major menu change as "being on top of its innovation game."* Fair enough. But never forget to focus on the basics. And that always starts with the customer experience. Is innovation serving the overall customer experience? If it is, excellent. If not, it deserves a rethink. Find out what they want and figure out how to deliver: *truth in action*. Context is constantly changing. What creates success may not over time be what preserves success. Does anyone remember TWA or Blockbuster? It's important to remember that innovation

---

* Since its beginning in 1965 Subway has been all about the customer experience. You tell the counter-person what you want, and they make it right there in front of you. Simple, but a bit time-consuming. The "innovation" discussed here ended that core emphasis by creating a menu from which customers are encouraged to order. Less customer involvement means speedier time in lines. Will it work? It won't be the CEO who decides. It'll be the customer. When it comes to innovation, who benefits? It's key to customer acceptance.

serves the needs of truth, not the other way round. The principles that support culture-driven leadership can't be applied selectively.

What the data tells us is that trust matters. It's a leadership cliché (but true) that people will fight more passionately for a cause if they have a significant stake in the outcome. As a leader, are you ensuring that the company culture rewards that investment every day and over time? We have seen already that trust can easily be lost, even when a leader (Howard Schultz and Starbucks) believes he has created an ideal worker-friendly culture. Time very quickly turns the most innovative innovation into yesterday's news. It's the "what have you done for me lately" paradox, right? It can seem like the more you do to create a great culture, the more that is expected, the less exceptional it can appear.

Truth is important for company culture. It's important for employees and it's important for customers. Telling the truth creates respect; it creates trust — and it ensures that the company's relationship with both is meaningful and sustainable. It simplifies your options and makes moving forward more straightforward. Remember, it doesn't matter one bit how you think you are doing. It doesn't even matter what your board or stakeholders think. What matters is what the customer thinks. How the brand is perceived. It doesn't mean the others can be ignored. But the customer always comes first.

Their loyalty. *Their* trust.

WHY THIS MATTERS

Consumers overwhelmingly insist that trust is the number one factor influencing the choices they make when purchasing goods and services. According to Edelman's "In Brands We Trust" global survey,[11] there are three main reasons why consumers trust brands: product experience, customer experience, and impact on society.

First, 87 percent of consumers interviewed cited their experience with a product as a reason for trusting a brand. Broken down further, 73 percent cited the quality of the product or service as the reason for their trust. When it comes to customer experience, 56 percent mentioned their customer experience with a brand as being important in creating trust.

Included within that category were things like how the company treats the consumer, how quickly it responds to complaints, and how well it protects clients' privacy. Finally, 38 percent of respondents listed a reason encompassing a company's impact on society, including how fairly it treats its staff (the largest factor in this category), but also things like the stance the business takes (if any) on wider social issues such as the environment and racial and gender equality.

According to a leading strategic branding and digital agency, brand trust[12]

- drives new business,
- increases marketing receptiveness, and
- creates loyalty.

Brand loyalty, meanwhile, "builds client and customer advocacy [for the brand], and advocacy and goodwill can help a business weather any storm."[13]

None of this will (should) come as a surprise. The thing is building and sustaining brand loyalty is extremely difficult. Sustaining it, particularly. This must be done on a daily (monthly and yearly) basis. Do you have the personality, the mindset, the will, and the commitment to accomplish this?

THE PROBLEM WITH TRUTH AND ACCOUNTABILITY

Fake news has been — ironically — in the news a lot over the last few years. The media is not trusted. Not long ago, we mostly accepted as true what we heard or read in the news. The media had authority. Today, the truth seems to have become whatever we want it to be, and generally, the only things deemed true are those that reinforce whatever it is we already believe.

The belief that there should be accountability for not telling the truth is still accepted and understood, but fewer and fewer people seem to be held to account.

Since 2018, the number of CEOs fired or forced to quit because of ethical misconduct (like bribery, fraud, or misrepresentation) has hit an all-time high. According to a Gallup survey, "business executives rank near the bottom on a list of professions by perceived ethics and honesty."[14] Trust is at all-time lows across the board. Is it any wonder that according to a recent survey "distrust is now society's default emotion"?[15] Only 37 percent of us trust social media, and trust in traditional media is down to 50 percent. "Without faith that our institutions will provide solutions or societal leadership," the report concludes, "societal fears are becoming more acute."[16]

In other words, we may trust business overall to do the right thing but not necessarily business leaders. The need to do better by winning back trust is not just a good idea. Trust in leadership is an imperative.

Why do so many distrust business leaders? Why is there such little faith in the integrity of the media or our political leaders? There is, it seems, a belief that amongst the leaders in all those fields there is a lack of principles.

Consider the following thought experiment: Let's say there are two friends at work. Each has an opportunity to steal a box of Keurig pods from work. They both decide against doing so. The first decides not to because they feel that the chances of getting caught are too high. It's too risky. The second feels that stealing is dishonest and, so, to take the pods would just be wrong. Okay, both did the "right" thing. Does it matter they each had a different reason for not taking the pods? The first didn't steal

> **Truth is important for company culture. It's important for employees and it's important for customers.**

them because they felt the risk of exposure was too great; for the second, it was a moral choice. Both decisions are justified: one might be considered pragmatic or practical, the other principled. Low road versus high road.

Remember: the results are the same. Does it matter why the two individuals made the choice they did? Should it? Do principles matter? Is it necessary for a leader to have principles? Are you the type of leader who takes the principled (high road) approach or the one who opts for the practical (low road)? It's a topic that gets discussed in limited ways in business schools and corporate seminars: *character.*

Character matters. We can argue all day how awful it is for people to steal, but that won't stop people from stealing. Bad actions may always take place, but they are less likely to do so in a culture that promotes truth and trust. And the culture-driven leader is responsible for creating that culture. As leader, it starts with you. It always will. You are the spark in the culture, and how the culture is communicated across the company has everything to do with who you are and how you embody and personify the culture. You can't wait until the hard decisions are being made to find out what kind of person you are. "Great … performers depend on deep reservoirs of technique and artistry; their art has less to do with the pressures of the moment than with all they've done to prepare for that moment."[17] In short, it comes down to character. CEO is a title; leadership is something far more abstract, but I believe *character* is at its core. Artists and actors spend years devoted to learning and practising their craft. When they reach a point where the hard work seems effortless in practice, that's the payoff. Same with true leadership. Effective leadership is all about mastering technique, and it requires time, experience, and dedication. And, I am convinced, the right character. An artist is true to their craft when they apply the full authority of their skills to their creative vision; a business leader also needs to be true to their craft, which, in our case, is leadership. It's our canvas.

> ## As leader, it starts with you. You are the spark in the culture.

What makes this issue so important for me is that as business plays a bigger and bigger role in society, its influence will grow proportionately. How businesses operate, the actions they take, will, therefore, have a huge impact on everybody's life. And that will have everything to do with who is running our businesses, and how. Sixty percent of employees expect CEOs, for instance, to "speak out on controversial issues they care about" and 80 percent — an impressive majority — "of the general population" want business leaders to be "personally visible when discussing public policy with external stakeholders or work their company has done to benefit society."[18]

Are we ready? Are *you* ready?

TRUTH OR CERTAINTY?

Both. A leader must be truthful; a leader also must project certainty. Maintaining balance while trying to do both is very difficult. There are no maps to tell you how to navigate that road. Ideally, a leader has created and sustains the kind of culture that accommodates circumstances when certainty needs to take precedence over truth — and vice versa. The sign of a damaged culture is the degree to which a leader loses control over the latter. Truth and certainty may shift positioning, but neither one should be ignored completely.

Leaders must make difficult decisions all the time, and it isn't always clear what the right decision is, or even what makes the "right" decision right. What if a decision that will make the shareholders happy will adversely affect your employees? or risk turning off your customer base? Deciding how to balance truth with certainty is an ongoing challenge for leaders.

A brand is a symbol of a company's commitment to truth. It says, "You should have 100 percent confidence in this product or service. You can trust us." It doesn't mean, "You can trust us … up to a point" or "this product is more or less what we promise it is." Imagine what would happen if every product or service was only paid for after the customer had a chance to test it. We don't pay for our dinner at a restaurant before sitting down to eat it. Don't companies trust us? How many company executives feel personally responsible for improving the customer experience? In my experience, the answer would be *occasionally, seldom, now and again*, or, far more likely, *hardly at all*. Most important, very few at executive levels even know what customer experience is or could profile a customer from first-hand experience. It's the kind of need that tends to be outsourced or solved via investment in technology.

For example, consider the Platinum Card from American Express. It carries a "no limit" spending allowance, but you have a pay-over-time option: when you buy something, they warn you that the amount must be paid after thirty days — there is no carry-over — but you're also told that if you don't, you must pay interest. They provide an option that lures you into taking on more debt. Hotels do the same thing. Not only do they have your deposit and credit card on file, they charge you an "amenities" fee when you check in. If you don't use them, you'll be credited. Customers feel like deadbeats in the process. So ... there *is always a* limit. This is all explained to you in frustratingly confusing small print: an approach that is completely at odds with the concept of customer satisfaction. Do they want to have their cake and eat it too? Amex wants to be a charge card company, but a lender, too? What is the brand impact of this for customers?

Another example. You probably have been asked recently by your bank to "take a few minutes" to fill out a customer service questionnaire (most likely of the online variety). They've made it easy for you by employing a 0–10 system that rates your level of satisfaction. But how many of us *really* feel that our complaints are being heard and — most important — being acted on? or that a five-minute survey where questions seem designed to elicit generic and easily tallied responses in any sense validates our experience as a customer? We are less individual customers to most businesses than we are part of a data set to be compiled for the purposes of analytics. In other words, no one really cares what you *the customer* thinks or what your experience means to you; what they want to know is how customer data is tracking or trending.

As I have said, in my tenure at ING Direct, I made it an absolute that we never create a product or service that came with any fine print. The irony is that this was so unusual in the banking sector it created a modest backlash: *no one believed us!* "You must be hiding *something*."

It was a great problem to have.

THE ART OF LEADERSHIP: FACT AND OPINION

In any mission statement, goal, or plan, there is a mixture of facts and projection. One can't have only facts; to speak of the future is, necessarily, to speak of something that you can't have complete certainty about. If the projections have no basis in fact, however, then the plan will be too risky and speculative. The art in leadership is finding the right balance and a workable cost-benefit and risk-reward foundation for the plan. Investors, employees, and customers all need to agree that the plan, the mission, is workable and will lead to success.

HOW TO BUILD TRUST

It shouldn't be that hard. What's hard is *keeping* trust. A company can't be open about the truth during the exciting early days of a business and then default to revealing it in fine print once they can get away with it. To create trust, it's necessary to tell the truth. It is just as important when a business enters a mature stage — and it remains true even in stage three.* The Gallup team not long ago came up with an interesting survey on trust in the workplace that included several "key competencies"[19] it deemed important to building trust.

The Seven Samurai of Trust

1. The ability to build relationships that establish connections that transmit ideas and accomplish work
2. A drive for development that focuses on followers' needs, expectations, and aspirations
3. Comfort with leading change in organizational strategy in alignment with the vision
4. The capacity to inspire others by encouraging their efforts and celebrating success
5. Critical thinking that seeks information openly, invites dissent, and stimulates debate where needed
6. Communication skills that result in clear, open, and transparent dialogue that empowers trust
7. A need for accountability to hold yourself and others responsible for performance

None of these should surprise, and all meet the common sense test. But how often do the cultures of our organizations embody all of the seven items? Context can be used as an excuse for settling for "kind of" hewing close to the letter. Over the long run, what do you want to be remembered

---

* Trust builds over time, of course; we don't trust people we hardly know, right? We save trust for the ones we know well, which is why betraying trust is so problematic in the second stage of a business where customer relationships are mature. It's a chestnut that it is cheaper keeping customers than going to the expense of finding new ones, and to keep customers you need to keep their trust.

for? And how? Rules of conduct, in order to work, must operate the same way the muscles do for a ballet dancer or track athlete. We can't stop and think each and every time we act or are required to make a decision. It must be a part of our muscle memory.

In another context, these were called "habits of the heart." It's not about what you do. It's about who you are. That's where it all starts.

"IT'S NOT A LIE ..."

When I was working my way through college, I had a summer job on a construction crew. As one might expect, I was the lowest of the low. I was doing everything from installing insulation and roofs to carpentry to hauling cement; basically, doing everything no one else wanted to do.

One day, we were sitting around the coffee truck with the crew. The foreman walked up and asked if anyone knew how to operate a backhoe. Without even thinking, I blurted, "Yup. I do." Truth is, I could barely operate a shovel.

"You serious?" he said.

"Yeah," I said. "No problem."

There must have been a dozen or more guys standing around, and they were all looking at me like my hair was on fire.

Bold as brass, I said, "What's the pay?"

That did it.

"One-seventy-five an hour," he said.

Well, that was fifty cents more than I was making at the time.

"Okay," I said.

He nodded, told me he would be back at the end of shift for a demonstration, and walked off. It was late in the day already, which was probably a good thing because I didn't really have that much time to think about what I was going to do.

I knew a guy on the nightshift and told him what I had done. I basically bribed him to give me a crash course in how to operate a backhoe. He either felt really sorry for me or admired my brass (or maybe both!), but he agreed to do what he could.

The next morning, the foreman showed up. I jumped into the backhoe and fired it up and did some basic manoeuvres that I had memorized from the night before. Anyway, we were about to get into some complicated moves when he suddenly signalled me to shut down. I figured he'd seen enough. *You're fired.* Instead, he said, "That's great." He was already walking away with some other crew to deal with another daily crisis.

In his eyes, I was who I said I was.

Remember the classic *Seinfeld* bit where George tries to rationalize his deceit by telling Jerry, "It's not a lie if you believe it"? The point is, at the moment that foreman asked if anyone knew how to operate a backhoe, I truly saw myself as that person. And I think that I have probably been doing the same kind of thing again and again in my life without really thinking that much about it. I learned to trust my instincts. How we see others has a lot to do with how we see ourselves. That's where it all starts.

> A leader needs to *be seen* leading.

I was well along into my banking career, and my colleagues and I were at a big conference. The speaker began his motivational presentation by waving a twenty-dollar bill and asking, "Who wants it?" I immediately jumped to my feet and strolled up to the front of the room and took it. Everyone laughed and clapped. Later, the speaker came up to me and said that in his many years of speaking at conferences, no one had ever taken the bait. I was the first. "Well," I said, "I hope you don't want your twenty bucks back."

A leader needs to *be seen* leading. The instinct can't be faked, however. It has to be like a muscle memory, not something you think about but what you do. Who you are. And you have to be able to back it up. Not just once, but every time.

THE UGLY TRUTH ABOUT WHO "GETS" TO BE LEADER

It would be the most wonderful thing in the world if each of us could end up doing exactly what we wanted to do and if each of us was justly compensated for our efforts and hard work. But we know that doesn't (often) happen.

Life is unfair. If there are ten people in the room, there will be one leader. If there are one hundred people in the room (or even a thousand or a hundred thousand), chances are there will still be only one leader. The odds of being that leader are long.

What does this mean? Just this: you have the make it happen. You have to seize the moment. *Carpe diem*, in other words: seize the day. No one is going to hand it over to you on a silver platter. *Leadership has to be seized.* The opportunity arises and the natural order is that someone has to step up and take it. Pure courage for the few. Children compete with one another to be king of the hill. It's about proving yourself and proving what you can do. It won't matter what you think you know or how much you think you deserve it. You have to step into the ring. And win.

CONCLUDING THOUGHT

Remember, telling the truth is a responsibility. As a leader, you need to be always stepping up and taking on that responsibility so that everyone in your organization will follow your example. There can't be a truth for you and another truth for them and still other truths for your customers.

Leaders are no different from anyone else: they tend to act — and react — too quickly, acting on impulse rather than taking whatever time is required to think a decision or action through. Our world has become real time. Everything is immediate and now. Nothing waits. This means there is little to no time to properly consider our opinions, our thoughts, what we say, our actions, and how we react. Every day, we react too fast and find out later that we were wrong. It's our world! The demand is that we react. There is no time for reflection. Be decisive means right now. For a leader, this creates a serious problem because the consequences of a wrong decision are manifold. George W. Bush famously answered, "I'm the decider," when questioned about his leadership role. It isn't, however, just about deciding; leadership is about making the *right decisions* — better: *judgments* — in an informed and timely fashion. It's better to let a decision sit until relevant facts are assembled and interpreted. Getting it right takes experience. There are two kinds of bad decisions: ones made too quickly and ones too-long delayed.

In my experience, the process of making the right and the timely decision begins with a commitment to the truth. It keeps things simpler. Not simple; it will never be simple.

ACTION POINTS

- Truth is a commitment to the mission that is understood and shared by everyone.
- The customer's truth matters more than your own.
- You are the brand; who people see is who you are.
- Never assume; check and check again. Confirm.
- Ask yourself, "Is this the right thing to do?" If you aren't sure, it probably isn't. If it isn't and you know it, don't pretend it is.

Chapter 7

WE WILL BE FOR EVERYONE

Creating a culture that accepts diversity, inclusion, and openness to everyone helps to focus activity on performance, the mission, and high customer-experience satisfaction. It says, "This is what we do. This is our product or service. If that's right for you, welcome. If not, thanks for stopping by." It doesn't mean that you are obligated to literally create services or products that appeal to everyone. The paradox of "being for everyone" means you won't be. What it means is, you could be. "We will be for everyone" just says we treat everyone the same, with the same product; we do not, for instance, create or improvise exceptions in efforts to accommodate one type of customer over another, change the price or level of service based on a customer's profile, or manipulate terms of service to prioritize preferments in any way. It's a fine line between identifying and finding customers and discriminating on factors that have nothing to do with a product or a service being offered. One product, one constituent style of service — start to finish — no exceptions. It's a point of view that has objective criteria, not subjective exceptions. It's the mindset of a culture-driven leader, which, by example, is communicated to everyone in the company.

Does it sound simple? As the famous quote goes, the devil is in the details.

. . .

In fall 2022, the telecommunications giant AT&T launched an advertising campaign that sounded a lot like "we will be for everyone." The ads featured NBA superstar LeBron James raving about the new iPhone Pro.

His AT&T partner on the ad agrees: "And you'll get our best deal."

James demurs. "But *everyone* should get it."

"Everyone *can* get it."

Back and forth they go.

"Every new customer?"

"Yes."

"Every existing customer?"

"Yes."

It sounds straightforward. When something sounds too good to be true, however, it's because it usually is. I am sceptical. We'll have to wait and see whether AT&T really has taken a giant step toward uncomplicating the wireless service market, or if this was an incentivized and "time-stamped" offer that will lapse.* In other words, where is the fine print?

HERE'S OUR PRODUCT AND PLAN … UNTIL IT ISN'T

Netflix was ad-free, with subscribers paying a basic flat rate, until October 2022, when the company announced its first tiered-subscription plan. Customers wishing to avoid advertisements could pay extra.

It's easy to understand why Netflix needed to introduce this change. It's Business 101. Everything has a cost or a consequence. Formerly alone at the top in the streaming services market, Netflix suddenly was facing incredible economic challenges from a host of aggressive competitors and declining market share (a serious context change). It's entirely possible that customers won't mind the increased fees for commercial-free streaming, or they may even accept commercials as still a good bargain. On the other hand, now

---

* We see more and more stories about cost-cutting companies being forced to revise customer-based loyalty points; it's a move necessary from the company's standpoint but hard to justify to "loyal" customers who earned the points.

operating inside an altered competitive environment, Netflix may slip toward its stage-three existence — the next Blockbuster or BlackBerry gone from the market.

Later in this chapter, we will consider the interesting legacy of Southwest Airlines. For now, keep in mind that Southwest's identity was tied to treating everyone the same. They had a new model that upended the aviation industry. Fares were too high. So, they came up with a low-cost fare that was the same for everyone; there was no special treatment for anyone and no extras. That has all changed, and Southwest is now essentially competing *with* and *not against* other passenger air carrier models.

Companies are always searching for ways to maximize profit. They have to keep in mind that investors, shareholders want the best return on their investments. Customers want the lowest price for the best value. That tension is universal, and companies need to find the best outcome in the middle — short term and long term. The basic (and constant) struggle that every company faces.

A key principle is *customer acceptance*. It sounds trivial, but the implications for ignoring it are profound. Customers might agree to a change, but that is not the same thing as acceptance. Initially, when customers subscribed to Netflix, there was one plan and one flat rate, no exceptions. Today, customers are being offered different plans for different services based on scaled payments. Existing customers have no choice other than to pay extra for what they used to get at a basic rate. There is actually a choice: they can find an alternative streaming service. What had been simple has become more complicated. What had been for everyone is now for everyone — but with conditions, incentives, and compromises and — critically — the potential for declining levels of customer acceptance and satisfaction.

"IN THE MIRROR" MOMENTS

Big insights often come in small packages.

On one of my first trips to Holland when I was with ING Direct, I was walking down a residential street in Amsterdam and noticed something odd. There were no curtains on the windows. When I mentioned this to a colleague, he gave me a puzzled glance. "Curtains? Why? We have nothing to hide."

It is a very interesting experience to have a cultural assumption blow up in one's face, and this seemingly simple experience ended up having a profound effect on me. I had just naturally assumed that we all had curtains on our windows, because we all had something to hide. But I think my Dutch colleagues had it right. The idea behind "we will be for everyone" is much harder to explain than the others, but it might help to think of your business — and you, as the leader — as having nothing to hide. More formally, it means creating a culture that accepts diversity, inclusion, and openness to everyone, a culture that helps to focus activity on performance and acceptance.

CASE NO. 1: SOUTHWEST AIRLINES — A NEW WAY OF DOING AN OLD THING

Founded by the flamboyant and unconventional Herb Kelleher in the 1970s, Southwest Airlines is today the world's largest "low-cost carrier." It will come as no surprise that few in the commercial passenger airline industry were happy with the arrival of no-frills budget carriers like Southwest, but founder Herb Kelleher — a true rebel in every sense of the word — didn't care. He wasn't concerned about what the industry thought; he cared about what his customers wanted. Fares were too high, and he had the lightbulb moment that customers were not happy about it. If the industry structured its fare system based on costly amenities and services, why not offer lower fares for fewer services. There have always been discount airlines, but none have ever executed their business plans well enough or survived long enough to be a force in the industry. Among Keller's first forays was a Houston–Dallas no-frills ticket for $13 (which was cheap even back then). And from 1973 to 2019, the company turned a profit every year by keeping their customers and employees happy. It wasn't only the cost-cutting, however, that attracted business. Kelleher had a nose for how to keep customers happy. His formula for success was simple: your employees come first. And if you treat your employees right, guess what? Your customers come back, and that makes your shareholders happy. Start with employees and the rest follows from that. Think of it as finding a new and reliable way of doing an old thing.

Could it really be that simple? Not in terms of commitment and leadership, no; but with the right kind of leader and the right culture? Yes. Kelleher died in 2019 at the age of eighty-seven. In 2022 Southwest Airlines announced it would "add a fourth fare category as part of changes designed to attract more business travelers and boost revenue."[1] A *fourth* fare category? If you thought you understood what a "low-cost" carrier was, you would be excused for assuming that a tiered-fare system on *budget* carriers was taboo — especially if that carrier was positioning itself as an affordable alternative to traditional carriers that depend on up-priced add-ons.

According to an industry analyst, "Airlines frequently tinker with fares and fees to squeeze more revenue from passengers."[2] That is undoubtedly true, but what is also true is that was not the Kelleher model. If you're in business, you confront tremendous pressure to grow the business and — important — *keep it growing.* If you follow everyone else, you'll be compared with everyone else — for good or bad.

> **Once the barricades have been stormed successfully, the revolutionaries are faced with the "what now?" question.**

It's interesting to imagine what Herb Kelleher would have done had he still been in charge in 2022. Would he have decided that his low-cost, no-frills passenger carrier model was no longer a profitable venture *in the current climate* (context)? Or would he have doubled-down on his "we will be for everyone" model and tried to find a way to compete? They were different; they had a strong culture based on disruption. And they were a huge hit!

The problem with any revolution, of course, is that once the barricades have been stormed successfully, the revolutionaries are faced with the "what now?" question. The management team at Southwest had a business that was hugely popular. Everyone (employees, stakeholders, investors) was happy and feeling confident and secure, profits were high, and customers loved them. And that's when the trouble started. Competitors who ignored them were now taking notice and imitating them, and experts and analysts who prophesied their demise were writing probing articles about what geniuses they were. Being the pioneer is fun at first, until other homesteaders arrive in droves and threaten to drive you off. Your range of movement — your operational elbow room — disappears. By successfully challenging the market and revolutionizing how business is done, you and your company have become the new target of those storming the barricades in the next revolution.

The point is, "we will be for everyone" cannot be a handy slogan. It has to be *believed* and *accepted*, not just by you and your team but also, most importantly, by the customer.

The goal in creating ING Direct, of course, was to appeal to customers who wanted higher rates on savings accounts than were available from traditional banking institutions. Having more money was a direct good. Our mission of "leading Americans back to savings," however, became a bigger picture greater good; it allowed and encouraged individuals — often for the first time in their lives — to be more financially self-sufficient, independent, and secure. The essence of building in a "we will be for everyone" culture is precisely finding expanded value far down river from the initial transaction.

In the case of Southwest, the airline admitted upfront its revenue-enhancing strategy was built on pursuing its wealthier, deeper-pocketed, and more important customers. It made perfect economic sense. I have no idea what the cost of this change in strategy has been to its culture, or to its employee and customer engagement. The culture-driven leader is bound to consider more than merely the economic impact of policies and strategies.

To start out with a great value proposition to customers (low price) is doable, but, eventually, you have to find a premium value that customers will keep buying. And what you have on offer has to be better than a competitor's value and pricing propositions for a customer to move or switch. It's the law of the marketplace. If one business model comes to resemble a competitor's in all ways except for cost, how long do you think it will be before even that difference is neutralized?

The question for leadership then becomes, "Will you shift or slow the growth and stay true to the mission?" Where once we had authentic alternatives, now we have companies that merely appear to be alternatives; we have choices between products we can't tell apart. What would Richard Branson have done? Was there a way to compete while staying true to the principles of "we will be for everyone"?

Responding to and dealing with competition and also attempting to "stay true" to customer commitments is very difficult, and in our increasingly globalized economy the magnitude of competition is off the charts. As we said, Southwest Airlines may have decided it had no choice. But what does making that choice say about the nature of leadership? Is context all that matters?

Rush to compassion, crawl to judgment.

CASE NO. 2: THE RICHARD BRANSON WAY

"The person who runs the company is critical," according to Virgin founder Richard Branson.[3] "If you choose somebody who genuinely loves people and looks for the best in people, that's critical. And if you bring someone in who isn't good with people then you can destroy the company very quickly."

The road to hell is paved with good intentions; no one sets out to fail. A leader can create a great culture, but that might not be enough. Richard Branson *is* Virgin culture. "Treat people as you'd want to be treated and they'll do their best work" might seem like a slogan dreamed up by the publicity department. When Branson claims he "genuinely loves people," it's easy to wonder about his sincerity. Does he really love people or is that just a cynical ploy to motivate? I don't think so. I think he's being honest. The thing is, on a practical level what difference does it make? A mindset and set of behaviours that is always putting the welfare of employees first doesn't necessarily help you create a company that can escape setbacks or stumbles.

I always want people working as hard as I do. Richard Branson wants the same, and at a very early stage of his career, he found a way to make it happen. "Praise employees instead of criticizing them." He believes it's important for leaders to be able to listen and to be genuinely receptive to input from everyone and — most important — "to act" on that input.

Generally speaking and whenever possible, we tend to respond better to encouragement than criticism. It's the carrot or the stick approach. Praise is important — we all need our carrots — but there are times when the stick is necessary in order for an employee to get up to speed or back on track. There is no easy path to knowing which is best. A leader needs to have the emotional intuition to know who he is dealing with, what they will respond to, and what needs to get done. Berating someone for not doing something they don't know how to do is not good leadership. Taking them to task for not doing what you hired them to do, however, is necessary. Too much praise can dilute its effect and even lead to complacency. Too much criticism, on the other hand, is demoralizing and creates doubt, low self-esteem, and frustration. It is also a toxic source of disruption for overall performance. As I like to say, rush to compassion, crawl to judgment. It's a balancing act. The reason I put such a high value in my own career on my track record for hiring the right people is that it means I don't have to use the stick very often. Frankly, having to admonish employees is in many ways a sign of your failure and not theirs.

THE RECRUITMENT DILEMMA

The reason I have spent so much time and energy in my career creatively vetting my recruitment choices is simple: when you take the time and make the effort to hire the best possible people, you end up spending a lot less time wielding the carrot or stick. "We will be for everyone" applies (as principles do) not just to the customer but to the people with whom you work. A rude fact of life is that while everyone is entitled to apply, only one will meet the criteria for selection. Work experience and a resumé are handy, but those often prove too "off the shelf" and simplistic. We now have recruitment software that can quickly filter so-called promising candidates from not-so promising ones. How do we define promising? And the automated approach strikes me as a bit like grabbing the closest apple in the barrel. They might look all the same, but are they? It's a real challenge, don't get me wrong.

One of the most obvious complexities faced in a business today is the very same diversity that in most ways is such a wonderful development.

I know what I want, but it's so much harder to know what the candidate wants! To be honest, when I started out the concept of a work-life balance simply didn't exist. Today, it's much different. We are looking at work-life-balance demands as a recruitment priority; finding the business-culture alignment between candidate and recruiter can be like playing a game of darts in the dark, and as more and more needs, preferences, considerations, or accommodations are added to the list, the challenge of finding the ideal candidate can seem daunting. The benefits of investing time and effort in recruiting, however, far outweigh the costs. Time or money saved at the front end, in my experience, can mean time lost and increased costs downstream.

At ING Direct, we had very high retention numbers. It wasn't only our customers who identified with our mission; our employees did too. And I think a big reason was that we threw as wide a net as possible looking for the right candidates. It was incredibly time-consuming and a lot of hard work, but worth it. That a CEO like Richard Branson, for instance, routinely attracts applicants in numbers well above the norm speaks to his culture-driven leadership acumen. His companies employ the best because his leadership attracts the best. Not the best resumé, the best *person*.

> **The benefits of investing time and effort in recruiting far outweigh the costs.**

The challenge today is discovering better and more effective recruitment strategies and techniques for attracting human beings and not just workers. In other words, the pressure is high to build longer and more time-consuming checklists, and that makes it even more difficult building (and sustaining) a strong and successful team.* The bigger the scale and size of a business the greater the complexity associated with team building. The more diverse and inclusive society is the more challenging it will be to get it right. Have we found a way forward?

---

* Which is a good reason to study, in-depth, successful companies like Richard Branson's Virgin. It isn't just hiring the right person but keeping them on board. A good brand with high employee retention and a successful culture will always attract the right talent.

NO CHILD LEFT BEHIND?

Remember No Child Left Behind, the education initiative from a few administrations ago? What about expanding that? What about No Customer Left Behind? What if every potential business leader made it a priority to seek out and address the needs of the customers who often get "left behind" as companies grow and adapt? Frankly, that doesn't seem to be an important part of our culture. We talk so much about business culture and culture-driven leadership (I should know), but what we tend not to talk about nearly enough is how easily context can pressure a culture in a way that might change a company's priorities. Culture does not operate in a vacuum. We can create a culture, but context shapes that culture. We say our customers are the number-one priority, but do we really mean it? Are we willing to put that commitment to the test every day? What about all the customers that don't fit the traditional profiles? How are we serving them and their best interests? Not our best interests, but theirs? How can you be for everyone if some are treated better than others? There is a never-ending opportunity to do better.

How can you be for everyone if some are treated better than others? There is a never-ending opportunity to do better.

I remember dropping into my old bank not long after we started ING Direct. The clerk recognized me. "We had one of your customers in here yesterday," he said. I asked him what happened. She had wanted to close her account and take the balance to ING Direct, he said. I laughed good-naturedly. "Oh, well, sorry about that." He wasn't bothered. It turned out the bank had been willing to match ING Direct's rate *at first*, but when he checked her balance, the bank decided upping her rate wasn't in the policy guidelines for rate ladders.

Wow. I still remember the huge smile I had on my face when I walked out. I think it might have been among the truly satisfying moments of my life.

DO THE MATH

It isn't easy to lead from the front, like Branson and Herb Kelleher. You are always at the front of the line, being appraised and being judged. And these days the scrutiny is non-stop. I bet there were more than a few times when even model leaders Branson and Kelleher felt inclined to just let things slide. When you hear the higher calling, however, it's what you do. And when you do it often enough, it gets to be a positive habit. There is a story told about Branson, that he was so concerned about the seven thousand candidates that had applied for one position that he went to the trouble of creating a video message to thank them. As a *Forbes* writer who profiled Branson commented, "It's the kind of personal touch that few CEOs would engage in and truly helps to set the company apart from its peers."[4]

It's difficult to put a number on the value of an act of kindness or generosity; being a decent human being and treating others as you want to be treated is its own reward. However, we can make an educated guess: it is estimated that there are on average about 150,000 candidates rejected for every one thousand jobs posted.[5] Taking the trouble to make rejected candidates feel highly valued means they will walk away with positive feelings about you and your brand.

A new way of doing an old thing, right? Finding customers is hard; retaining customers over time is even more difficult. A brand is what people are saying behind your back: make sure as the leader that you are improving your brand every day. It starts and ends with customer experience.

THE NEED FOR NEW LEADERSHIP: OPPORTUNITY

The traditional source of stability in economic life — the middle class — is falling behind financially and is "no longer the majority," according to the most recent research. The concern for any culture-driven leader who values the principle of "we will be for everyone" is the risk of defining out of existence those who don't seem to matter. We are living through a time when families in the most prosperous countries of the world are struggling to afford even the basics: food, housing, health care, education, and so on. Two million people — *including more employed people than ever* — used food banks in March 2023 alone in Canada, "a 32 per cent increase from the same month the previous year and more than 78 per cent higher than in March 2019."[6]

It seems to me our need today is not just new and better leadership, but new and better leadership where it really matters. Consider the following statistics:[7]

- One in three small- and medium-sized Canadian businesses are planning to invest in software in the next twelve months.
- Tech-sector growth was about 22.4 percent for the period 2021–2024.
- Over half (55 percent) of tech entrepreneurs are struggling to hire the employees they need.

The point is not to criticize the obvious benefits for the economy innovations in the tech industry offer. What should concern us are the consequences of what we are investing in. Who is being served? And why?

"After more than four decades of serving as the nation's economic majority, the American middle class is now matched in number by those in the economic tiers above and below it."[8] Middle-income Americans "have fallen further behind financially," research concludes, as "aggregate household income has substantially shifted from middle-income to upper-income households." Some 90 percent of the value of stocks owned by households is held by the wealthiest 10 percent of Americans, according to Federal Reserve data.[9]

It's not hard to figure out that a shrinking middle class is not good for the economy or for the country. The increasingly widespread middle-class anxiety about further losses is unquestionably contributing (in part) to our increasingly polarized outlook. Where will we find the leaders and the leadership style that will address and solve this challenge? How do we unite a society that appears determined to remain divided? How is the dilemma being addressed? As far as I can tell, not at all. When it comes to a serious issue like the disappearance of the middle class, we have entered an almost total leadership and/or entrepreneurial void.

Great leadership doesn't require a crisis, but it helps. A crisis can reveal opportunities that otherwise might remain hidden. It is a time for great leadership to emerge. A Lincoln or a Churchill understood this intuitively. There is never a time that will not reward effective leadership. The question is whether the leader in question is up to the task. What this means for us is that we face a period of enormous opportunity for emergent leadership.

A SOMETIMES BUMPY ROAD TO "EVERYONE"

When we started to build a new kind of culture at ING Direct in Canada, we backed into the "for everyone" idea. As we know, banks generally pay higher interest rates on larger deposits.

> **Great leadership doesn't require a crisis, but it helps.**

From the bank's perspective, it makes sense. The cost of administering larger accounts is lower, and having more of such accounts creates a bigger money supply for lending. The problem, of course, is that the bank is telling its customers that everyone is welcome, but the reality is, rich depositors *are more welcome* than modest or small depositors.

Well, if that was how the conventional financial services were doing it, we decided that we would do the opposite. Forget tiered rates of interest: one rate for everyone, and no exceptions.* We made it clear we would not offer higher rates to richer clients. As I have said, it created some interesting challenges.

We had several customers who tried to open accounts with a deposit of a single penny. I can hear those calls even now with their "gotcha" cheap thrill approach. "But your ads say no minimum!" For the ING Direct experiment to work, I would explain, we needed customers who were *serious about saving.* I always tried to end a tough call on a positive. "If you change your mind about becoming serious about saving, we'll be here. Put that penny in a jar. Do that every day for a year and come back. We'd love to get you started."

---

* The details of how ING Direct was organized should be (I hope) familiar by now.

The most fun I had was turning down entitled customers who threw tantrums and could not understand why we wouldn't agree to a preferred rate.

"But that's the rate for normal customers. What's *my* rate?"

I said it's the same for everyone. "Even for me, and I'm the CEO." I turned them down.

"You're making a big mistake."

When ING Direct debuted in the United States, we launched our "leading Americans back to savings" campaign with a splash: TV commercials, billboards, and social media — the works. From the get-go we were inundated with questions. Many were great, a few were not. Didn't matter: we had to answer them all.

"But what do we say?" the associates asked. It had been important in the early days of ING Direct to empower the associates with the authority to make decisions; no pushing the caller into the higher branches of the customer-service tree. No minimums, no fine print, no exceptions. But saying "no" is not easy. Especially in those very early days, everyone was energized and anxious to please. We gathered everyone into a huddle. I had a simple message: stick to the script. It's who we are. Tell customers how it works, and why it works. If they want exceptions or to do something we don't do, thank them for their interest, but tell them "no."

The everyday challenge was finding the balance between being for everyone but staying firmly inside the guard rails that defined and protected the service or product and its integrity. In short, the customer is always right if what's being asked is what has been promised.

CONCLUDING THOUGHT

We were for everyone — everyone who was serious about saving — but that didn't mean everyone was for us. I was more than okay with that. It's been estimated that 80 percent of New Year's resolutions have been dropped by the second week of February.

Commitments are easy to make, hard to fulfill.

ACTION POINTS

- The paradox of "being for everyone" means you won't be. What it means is, you could be.
- Treat everyone the same, with the same product.
- Exceptions are like the fine print that no one reads. It means you are not really doing what you say you are.
- One product, one constituent style of service — start to finish — no exceptions.
- "No" is a powerful tool when applied correctly and consistently.

Chapter 8

OUR MISSION IS TO HELP IMPROVE LIVES

For a healthy, vibrant society, financial security, the ability for all to be independent and free, is essential. Improving lives means helping to achieve this for all stakeholders, not just the lucky few, the privileged, or the elites. Having choice is fundamental to a better future for all. The key is "service to others." It could be anything; it could be many things. It needs, however, to be an "others-directed" purpose and a goal to which you are committed.

• • •

No matter the business, the culture-driven leader is always searching for a *broader* mission. Service to the greater good is inspiring and justifies many of the hard decisions we have to make for our work and personal lives.

We all want to feel that our labour is valued and that what we do has a larger meaning and purpose; in a previous chapter, we called it the "well-invested" promise. We all want to look back on what we've done with pride and a sense of real accomplishment. Pride not just in personal success but in having played a part in making society a better place. It doesn't always happen, of course, which is a big reason why culture-driven leadership needs to be rediscovered. We need an ongoing dialogue about the mission, and why we are working on a mission. A mission is a living thing that needs a constant supply of air to thrive. It needs ongoing dialogue in the open! And the mission needs to be tied to purpose. Yes, we need to have meaning and purpose; otherwise, we are just so many hamsters on a wheel. A culture-driven leader can connect the dots and pull the "broad mission" narrative together. Building a culture that values the mission and the service to others will be self-reinforcing and self-sustaining. Helping improve lives is a commitment that starts with a *living* culture.

WE ALL WANT SOME SUNSHINE

"Where do you work? What do you? How do you like it?" The response everyone wants to hear is, "It's a great company to work for!"

It's the simplest thing in the world. What do we all want? It comes down to one thing: we all want some sunshine.

YOU ARE ALWAYS IN THE SPOTLIGHT

Companies are continually in the process of being evaluated — by the market, by the stakeholders and shareholders, by customers, by the media, and (most critically) by everyone who has worked for, wanted to work for, or is working for the company. The brand and its reputation are what I called above a "living" concept; it is constantly evolving, either improving or diminishing (or often moving back and forth) over time.*

Staying in touch with the state of a brand and its reputation is critical; as a leader you always want to be ahead of problems coming up so you will have the time required to *react and repair* before a crisis turns the corner on critical. How do you do that? The answer is amazingly simple. *Walk around.*†
Talk to everyone inside and outside the company. Secretaries know a lot.

---

* Remember the Robert Iger example from an earlier chapter? He stepped down from Disney and turned the reins over to a hand-picked successor. Unfortunately, the brand suffered under the new boss's tenure and employees and shareholders revolted; the CEO was deposed and Iger was induced to return for a second shot at restoring the brand to its former glory.

† People never believed me when I said I did this on a regular basis. They thought it was a clever stunt. It wasn't.

Frontline service people know a lot. Drivers and security guards know even more. Your personal brand and your company's reputation are the summary of what's said behind your back. It doesn't matter what you think your company is doing to "improve lives"; your customer needs to believe it, and that means they need to trust you. Is that happening? Do you as leader know how to build trust with your customer?*

TRUST BUSTERS

Imagine there is a knock on your front door. You answer, and it's a stranger — a nondescript man — who politely asks if he can speak to your ten-year-old son *alone*. If you're like most people, you would automatically slam the door shut and call the police. It's the *reasonable* and *responsible* response. Nothing is more important to a parent than to protect their child. And yet, it was only recently that a Facebook whistle-blower disclosed that the world's most popular social media platform "knew social media usage could be harmful to kids, particularly for teenage girls."[1]

At the moment, there are more than fifteen thousand apps available on Amazon Appstore targeted at children.[2] The world of social media (especially the incredibly lucrative segment directed at children and adolescents) has been mostly unregulated. And, as we are learning, it can be harmful. No wonder, then, that an increasing number of tech leaders are admitting to having either banned or restricted their own children's access to computers and smartphones.

Regulation and safeguards designed to deal with this problem have been slow to follow. Recently, California passed Hippocratic oath legislation requiring "social media companies to make sure new products won't be harmful to minors." Is that enough? Who is making the decision about what we are exposed to, and why? Who benefits?

Tech companies are not evil; neither can they claim to be innocent, though. In the hugely competitive globalized tech market, accelerated development and

---

* We've all responded at some point to "customer surveys." These days, surveys are almost all conducted online and feel extremely impersonal. You end up feeling like you're sending your answers into a void. The point is, do we really feel we are being listened to? Do we really feel our opinions and experiences matter?

delivery-to-market speed are prioritized; the industry as a whole ignores or "back-burners" the risks and consequences of many of their products (like privacy and personal data autonomy). Profits depend on being first. Given that, it's fair to question if the "do no harm" prohibition has been incorporated into the industry's cultural DNA. How could that be judged? How do we define "harm"? Who decides? And how? What measures or mediations are appropriate to ensure that harm is not done? China recently legislated strict controls related to social media access for children and teenagers. In a so-called free society, who should have the right to access content? How free should speech be?

Obviously, it isn't just software developers and social media platforms caught in the crosshairs of the spirited debates about how to balance what's good for business with what is best for the public at large. In the financial services sector, agents (bankers, brokers, et cetera) have what's called a fiduciary duty to their clients, which means that agents are required to act on behalf of the client's best interests. This doesn't seem an extraordinary expectation. Shouldn't a financial advisor *always* be acting in my best interests? The question is, whose best interests should business leaders be acting for? Shareholders? Employees? Customers? What happens when the best interests of one group are in conflict with the best interests of another? Whose interests trump those of the other groups? It's complicated. In business — as in life —we face difficult and increasingly complex questions and there are no simple answers; there never are, of course, but that doesn't mean we can simply shrug our shoulders and pretend the problem will go away. It can't be "business as usual."

> Everyone is watching you ... *all the time*. There are no time outs or "do overs."

My passion for culture-driven leadership is not just PR; leadership dedicated to improving people's lives is not a slogan.* It works, for one thing,

---

* The problem for so much leadership today, in fact, is just that problem: culture-driven leadership has become a slogan with nothing of substance to consistently sustain it over time (from context to context).

consistently. It's reliable, defendable, and can be sustained over time in ways that fashionable or trendy strategies aren't. Why that's important, I hope, will become clear in what follows.

We have arrived on the shores of a "brave new world," and just like *The Tempest*'s Miranda, we are awestruck and "wonder" at the "beauteous" marvels that have appeared. In these, however, we confront unforeseen and unexpected dangers. We are, in other words, all Mirandas; we see the world changing right before our eyes, incredible and amazing, but not knowing whether that is in the long term good or bad. As business leaders we need to deal with the *consequences* of our actions.

OFF-THE-SHELF LEADERSHIP IS NOT AN OPTION

The stakes in the "serving the interests of our customers" derby couldn't be higher. According to a recent survey, 70 percent of consumers "want to know what the brands they support are doing to address social and environmental issues," while nearly half of respondents (48 percent) say that when buying a product they "pay close attention to a brand's social responsibility efforts."[3] Companies and their leaders are subjected to intense scrutiny; public expectations are high. Meeting those can be very difficult, even at the best of times.

We have become blasé about how comprehensively our world has been transformed by technological innovations. Increasingly, however, we are being made aware of emergent consequences from all that innovation. Dealing with all of those is a daunting task. No surprise, then, that a common default response is assuming that if we just wait long enough, a solution will turn up.[*] Technology created the problem, and technology can fix it.[†]

Leadership is built, trained, nurtured and — most important — *tested*, not once, but many times and across shifting contexts. It doesn't just show up ready to go. It's a reason why we put so much emphasis in culture-driven

---

[*] Interestingly, as you read this, ChatGPT is writing a job posting and a candidate is using ChatGPT to answer and apply. How can we know the impact of this?

[†] Remember the quote from T.S. Eliot from an earlier chapter about our "mechanized" culture and the need for human solutions to human problems?

leadership on character. Consider these stats: an overwhelming percentage of us believe "there is a skills gap"; 35 percent believe the skills gap "affects them personally"; and 40 percent believe "changing skills requirements will have the biggest impact on their job over the next five years."[4] It's a lot like a contractor starting a big renovation at your home and admitting to not having the tools and experience necessary to complete the job.

What does this mean for leadership? For something to happen — for something to get done — remember, *someone needs to make it happen*. A skills gap isn't just a problem at "this" or "that" rung on the ladder; it's important at every level. We are so accustomed to young and successful tech CEOs, for instance, that we confuse *real leadership* with success. It's like the amateur who wins big on their first hand of poker. The house knows better. It isn't about winning in the short term. The principle that we are in business to improve lives is a long-term commitment. The value of culture-driven leadership is in creating an environment where leadership and shared values are aligned over time and context. Helping customers improve their lives, and not just for now but for as long as possible. We all make mistakes. What we need are leaders who make the right choices when it really counts. It's how we create loyalty. It's how we improve lives.

> **Consequences need to be anticipated and managed; they are real and affect outcomes.**

By this point in our exploration, it should be clear that the marketplace of today looks like a foreign country compared to even a decade ago. The need for outstanding leadership is greater as well. From where I sit, the response to the challenge of finding and nurturing new leaders is a worrisomely short-sighted "business as usual."* Do we have the leaders with the necessary skills to navigate this new terrain? Will we? According to a Northeastern University study, 58 percent of companies surveyed report that their number-one strategic priority is closing the current leadership

---

* No flying above the clouds with most new leaders today! The 2023 collapse of Silicon Valley Bank and the trials (literal) of entrepreneurs like Sam Bankman-Fried come to mind.

skills gap. And 84 percent expect "they will experience a shortage of skilled leaders in the next five years."[5] Will we have the leaders? Whose future will it be? Will it be for everyone or just some of us?[*]

MAKING LIVES BETTER ... OR JUST MAKING MORE STUFF?

A recent commercial from a major telecom featured a customer — a man in his late thirties or so — entering a store. He looks incredibly embarrassed. Why? Hidden inside the bag he is carrying is *last season's* smartphone. The customers around him react with comic horror. A shocked mother even cups her hands over her innocent child's ears. I laughed when I first saw it, of course. Who wouldn't?

Here's the thing: no one asks the customer if the phone *still works* or if it's meeting his needs. No one asks him what reason he might have for wanting to spend hundreds of dollars on a new phone if the old phone is perfectly fine. The representative doesn't even bother to sell the customer on any advantages of a new phone. All that matters is that his phone *isn't the latest model.*

Whose interests are being served here? The customer's? Or the company's? Since its debut in 2007, there have been thirty-three distinct iterations of the iPhone. There are around 298 million smartphone users in the United States,[6] which represents about 90 percent of the population. It may be true that improved processing capabilities have made each iteration of the smartphone *marginally* more productive, but, as one industry source remarked, "Flagship phones are giving us only incremental improvements, and our upgrade culture is making less and less sense."[7] The result is, in a market saturated with smartphones, manufacturers need to find compelling reasons for consumers to upgrade; otherwise, sales will plummet, and profits will tumble. We circle back to our original question: How is this making a customer's life better?

So, new is not always better ... or so much better that the old needs to be discarded immediately. Still, phone manufacturers spend a lot of money convincing people that they do need the latest phone. Prices for smartphones, for instance, soared by 10 percent in the final quarter of 2021, "the fastest

---

[*] The skills gap problem has only been exacerbated by the enormous loss of labour that resulted in the so-called Great Resignation that began in 2021.

price increase to date."[8] Overall, in fact, smartphone prices rose 6 percent in a one-year period, according to a study not long ago.[9]

Who is being left behind? While we want to be inclusive, the very new innovations are creating ever bigger gaps in society. Unfortunately, not everyone is as lucky as our poor friend from the commercial. "In the year 2020, a smartphone is seen more as a necessity than a luxury — going without one means missing out on the many advantages to be had with internet connectivity in your pocket. But for billions of people around the world, owning a smartphone is still out of reach."[10] As many as 2.5 billion people live in countries where the average cost of a smartphone represents "a quarter or more of their monthly income."[11]

It's not news that we are addicted to our smartphones, and studies confirm that children and young people are cognitively evolving differently because of it. It doesn't make much sense, does it, to make our phones smarter if that means we all become dumber as a result? The point is, we as leaders have to be thinking of not just what is good for us as a company and what will make our shareholders happy; we need to know the short- and long-term consequences of what we are doing. What we know now is what we didn't know (or didn't really care to know) before: our choices matter. If we want leadership that

> **Whose interests are being served? The customer's? Or the company's?**

is more socially responsible, we need to know how that is happening and what it means. We need always to be having discussions about benefits versus costs, profits versus consequences. Leaders in today's challenging landscape can't escape taking stands. If they don't, stands will be forced on them. We have to do a much better job of knowing how and why we are doing what we do, and that will be an enormously big challenge for leaders of tomorrow, because more and more it's not enough to hide behind the "free choice" argument. When it comes to people's lives, it's about making the right choices.*

---

* Precisely the reason so many tech innovators monitor their own children's tech access and usage. If it's not good for your own children, why is it good for everyone else's?

WE DESERVE BETTER

Nothing lasts forever, right? One of the most challenging experiences of my life was watching the restructuring of ING Direct that culminated in its absorption by Capital One 360, the online arm of Capital One, in 2013. The unique and very special relationship we had built with our customers came to a slow end. It was back to banking "business as usual." I was discouraged and broken-hearted. I had staked my career on doing banking *different*. And we had succeeded!

Why does this matter?

In early 2024, the financial services giant Capital One announced it would buy Discover Financial Services for $35 billion. Consider this: in the fourth quarter of 2023, "Americans held $1.13 trillion on their credit cards, and aggregate household debt balances increased by $212 billion, up 1.2 percent," according to the latest data from the New York Federal Reserve.[12] It could be argued that making credit available to people helps them make purchases they couldn't make otherwise. True, but at what cost (literally)? As consumers run up their card balances, they "are also paying higher interest rates. The average interest rate on a bank credit card is roughly 21.5 percent, the highest it's been since the Federal Reserve started tracking the data in 1994."[13]

All good news for credit card companies. As one article noted, "Capital One has long had a business model looking for customers who will keep a balance on their cards, *aiming for customers with lower credit scores* than American Express or even Discover [Financial Services]"[14] (my emphasis). But is it a good deal for consumers? After battling inflation for more than two years, many lower- and middle-income Americans have run through their savings and are increasingly running up their credit card balances and taking on personal loans.

I've said that ING's mantra was "leading Americans back to saving." I believed in it as a principle. Always have, and I still do. My point here is not to hammer credit card companies. The fact that a credit card company has built its success on seeking out customers with low or poor credit scores, however, makes me wonder in what meaningful sense they care about their customers and their financial well-being. It has to be about something more than profits. What's the cause? Who benefits? How are lives being improved? Will we judge our time served as having been worthwhile?

We talk about a leader as a rebel with a cause. Making change always requires the building of a new culture within the context of an older and more orthodox culture. Improving people's lives requires commitment; making change isn't easy. You don't have to care about the needs of your customers, of course. If you want to focus on other priorities, that's fine. It's a judgment the culture-driven leader has to make, however, and has to keep making: Are you continually evolving the business to meet the needs and the best interests of the customer? It could be in big ways or small. For the culture-driven leader, what's important is having that broader mission always guiding your efforts.

THE BIG IDEA: IT'S NOT ABOUT SIZE, BUT IMPACT

It's easy to think that the goal of improving people's lives requires a huge and game-changing event or innovation. No, it's not about the size of an improvement or innovation but the overall impact. Does it represent a substantive improvement from a previous iteration? That is the motivation behind the principle. It could be — it often is — something small, something seemingly unnoteworthy. I said that our cafés weren't about coffee. They weren't. We went to all that expense and effort for something incredibly simple: an improved banking experience. Sit down, get comfortable. Have a cup of coffee. Oh, and did you have a question about your account? No problem. Relax.

A commitment to improving lives doesn't have to be your mantra. A culture-driven leader, however, needs to be motivated by something more than money. Whatever it is, it needs to be your cause. It may seem a paradox that so much of my career has benefitted from innovations in digital technology, but my cause is people-driven. My concern for the years ahead and the challenges we face is losing touch with how we do what we do. Surveys tell us, for instance, that 71 percent of Americans are nervous about being replaced by AI. "As many as 300 million full-time jobs around the world could be automated in some way by the newest wave of artificial intelligence."[15] Meanwhile, in late March 2023, "more than 1,000 technology leaders and researchers, including Elon Musk" signed an open letter urging "artificial intelligence labs to pause development of the most advanced systems, warning in an open letter that AI tools present "profound risks to society and humanity."[16] According to the letter, AI developers are "locked in an out-of-control race to develop and deploy ever more powerful digital minds that no one — not even their creators — can understand, predict or reliably control."[17]

I have not the slightest doubt that AI can (and will) be a tremendous benefit to mankind in many ways. My concern is that in the relentless drive to humanize machines we risk demoting humans to machine status. We risk, in other words, becoming the tools of our tools. Deciding what it means to improve lives, for instance, and how this can be achieved will never be more important than in the next couple of dec-

> **Are you continually evolving the business to meet the needs and the best interests of the customer?**

ades, especially for leaders who will be at the front lines in how this drama plays out. Remember, culture-driven leadership is about the "how" of what we do. That "how" is the culture. The most familiar question we all hear is "What do you do for a living?" A culture-driven leader might wonder "*Why* do you do what you do for a living" or "*How* do you do it?" I know why I do what I do. How about you?

HOW TO HELP IMPROVE LIVES

Companies today are being "encouraged" to engage directly with issues of justice related to race and gender, religion, identity, and with the health of the environment, and many other causes and issues. "Customers, especially millennials and Gen Z," according to one expert,[18] "are holding brands to a higher social standard than ever before. People overwhelmingly prefer to buy from companies that share their beliefs and values."

This wasn't always the case. Not that long ago, the idea that a business or corporation had any role to play in society other than delivering higher profits for shareholders was not the mainstream philosophy. The Nobel Prize–winning economist Milton Friedman famously dismissed completely the idea that business had any "social responsibilities" other than to "make as much money as possible while conforming to their basic rules of the society."[19] Business leaders, he reasoned, "are very poorly equipped when it comes to enacting social change."

Times have changed, though, and the business sector is responding to the new expectations of its customers. "Brands appear eager to demonstrate care for their customers and employees, and given the massive wave of social unrest, it's natural for them to want to appear as compassionate allies."[20]

> Culture-driven leadership is about the "how" of what we do.

The bad news is business might lack the experience and expertise necessary to fulfill the role of agent of change. Consumers "are sensitive to tone-deaf or empty statements, and there's no shortage of blunt criticisms online." We're all familiar with "greenwashing," a term describing an effort or product that is advertised as being environmentally friendly when it isn't.

It's clear that many executives today are not well equipped to deal with issues of social responsibility. What's obvious is that increasingly they have no choice: the role is being forced on them whether they like it or not.* For instance, in 2019 corporate pledges topped out at $450 million to "groups committed to social and racial justice."[21] The Ford Foundation, meanwhile, pledged an additional $520 million in grants for similar causes the same year, and stated the company would "borrow $1 billion so that it can substantially

---

* In 2022 beleaguered Disney CEO Bob Chapek found himself in hot water for not doing enough to defeat a controversial "Don't Say 'Gay'" bill sponsored by Florida's governor. It was a classic case of "damned if you do, dammed if you don't." No one accused of Disney of being anti-LGBTQ. Its crime was not taking an active and public stand against the bill. The governor and his allies, on the other hand, went to war against Disney once the company was compelled to apologize for not having taken sides sooner.

increase the amount of money it distributes."[22] The company's strategy was to "borrow money, spend it quickly and inspire others to follow Ford's lead."

Milton Friedman would have considered this as business and behavioural heresy. Today, it's more and more common. Even obligatory. The challenge for leadership is figuring out how to define the corporate message to fit the expectations of consumers and deciding how far a company's obligations extend. Leadership today faces a challenging balancing act: being both "socially responsible" and meeting internal company-specific goals and outcomes. Encumbering a mission statement with too many add-ons could risk pushing a company outside its abilities and expertise. "There seems to be a reckoning on social media, where it has become harder to ignore political topics or performatively share a hashtag to signify support. Consumers, many of whom have donated hundreds of dollars to these causes, are asking for more, and they've made it clear that corporate praise will be harder to come by — especially if organizations are not transparent in their commitments and hesitant to open their purses."[23]

Bottom line: the Milton Friedmans of the world did not have to worry about all this; the Bob Chapeks do. For a leader, making the right choice, the right commitments, supporting the right causes, adopting the right public profile while avoiding toxic blowback and backlash is becoming harder every day. But what about your stakeholders and stockholders? Your employees? Where do they all fit in this new hierarchy of obligations?

THE BROADER MISSION

It's tricky, no doubt about it. Leaders are tasked with the twin responsibility of navigating the daily dramas of the present and also of forecasting into the future. We have to be more right than wrong, but ultimately, we cannot escape our limitations of being trapped in the present. We just don't know. Context is changing not by the year or even by the month but by the hour.

The utility value of culture-driven leadership is its ability to create a business ecology based on principles rather than crystal balls. Principle-based culture is open to and allows for (and even encourages) adaptation and renewal. No matter the nature of the work nor the size of the business, it helps if the culture has a *broader mission*. In the simplest sense, the broader mission is what one finds "above the clouds." It answers the question, "Why does the company exist and what role can I play it making that happen?" There is no such thing as only one way to make society a better place for everyone. It can (and does) happen in millions of small ways. But they all add up.

As we said at the beginning of this chapter, we all need to have meaning and purpose. Building a culture that is based on values, the mission, and service to others will be self-reinforcing and self-sustaining.

GREAT PRINCIPLES SHARE THE SAME DNA

I said at the beginning of this book that all the principles share a great deal in common; they all share the same DNA.

For instance, a culture focused on helping improve lives puts a lot of effort into listening and simplifying. Hear what your customers want and do all you can to deliver. It only makes sense! "The definition of genius," wrote Albert Einstein, "is taking the complex and making it simple." ING Direct was a really simple idea. Help people feel good about saving. Another company with a simple idea: Deak International.

I served as president and CEO of Deak International, a foreign exchange and commodity business headquartered in New York, from 1985 to 1993. Deak provided merchant and investment banking services, and through Deak International provided foreign exchange and precious metals trading and refining services. I was given the huge challenge of completely reorganizing its operations, which meant relaunching a revitalized company in April 1986. I expanded the company from 52 to 192 branches worldwide, at the same time increasing its staffing from 350 to 1,500 employees.

The "under the hood" reality of the business itself was extremely complex. The core idea, however, was gorgeously simple (a reason why revenues climbed to $1 billion wholesale and $2.5 billion retail, and income grew to $70 million). It enabled individuals or businesses in one country to transfer funds to other countries.* It seems so simple today, but it wasn't then. Language barriers created problems, but what really created complexity was the labyrinthine networks of domestic and international financial regulations. Navigating those wasn't easy, believe me. And, of course, we had to deliver.

Security, ease of service, reliability had to be assured. Having and maintaining those became our bedrock appeal. They were essential for our reputation. Accepting responsibility for transferring millions of dollars at a time thousands of miles was a tough sell, like day-old sushi. We had to be there as solid as a rock. Any hitch or hiccup and we would be out of business in a flash.

> **Principle-based culture is open to and allows for adaptation and renewal.**

Deak's slogan was "Around the corner, around the world."

For the customer, our service was making dealing with foreign countries and currencies as easy and familiar as doing business in their own neighborhood. We had to listen, and we had to simplify. Our customers came to us because we made it simple for them. In a larger and more important sense, however, we also improved their lives. In short, our service meant there was one less "problem" for them to worry about. Our obligation was to focus on the end result and immunize the customer from having to deal with the complex details.

One wish I have for this book is to encourage as many readers as possible to demythologize the "innovation" process. We have apps to do just about everything. But there are a lot of things we need that are not being and will never be served by apps. Let's broaden our understanding of what innovation might mean. And that could start by simply looking at what you do every day and asking yourself, "Is there a better or simpler way to do it?" Scale your innovation thinking down to a more manageable (even a non-technological) level. Be aware and attentive to the architecture of process *all the time.*

---

* It's hard to imagine today that transferring funds internationally was ever a problem. It was, however.

Right now, I bet you could look around you and discover at least five things that people are doing that with modest refinements could be done better and more efficiently. It's what the culture-driven leader does all the time.

CONCLUDING THOUGHT

Our mission as leaders is to be the instrument that consistently and reliably directs and drives the company to achieve the desired outcome, which is to improve people's lives. If you're making your shareholders happy but ignoring your customers, it won't take long for your shareholders to find out about it. When the culture-driven leader says, "We're here for you," you and everyone who works with and for you has to believe it. Most important, your customers have to believe it.

Are we improving the quality of a customer's life?

ACTION POINTS

- Staying in touch with the reputation of your brand is critical; as a leader you always want to be ahead of problems.
- The goal of "improving lives" should include all stakeholders, not just the lucky few, the privileged, or the elites.
- Leadership is a synergy of short-term decisions and long-term judgments.
- Your leadership ultimately will be judged on who you are (what you have made for others), and less on what you have made yourself.
- Quality of life comes in many different sizes. Culture-driven leadership is all about finding as many as you can.
- The metric that indicates success in achieving the goal of improving lives is customer buy-in.

Chapter 9

WE WILL NEVER STOP ASKING WHY*

Asking why will enable you to identify the weak link in any system or process. If everyone on a team is encouraged to question, finding an answer or solution becomes easier. Being aware of other possibilities energizes and helps to build buy-in from everyone. It's not one person, it's everyone looking for answers together. A consensus of why gives everyone permission. As with all the principles, the buy-in to never stop asking why has to be incentivized and valued across the board.

. . .

It's human nature to become irritated when someone constantly questions everything. Just ask the average parent with a child in the why phase of development. It's not surprising, then, that creating a culture that inspires us to ask why is very difficult. Dealing with constant questioning can be frustrating and exhausting, and incredibly time consuming. Putting everything up for discussion can also become a point of friction and frustration; asking why might be misconstrued as objection to an action, or doubt about

---

* This chapter and the one that follows are intimately linked and could profitably be thought of as continuous. I have broken them up purely for convenience.

the merit of a decision. It might be seen as a strategy for creating roadblocks to progress. A productive culture uses why-based reasoning that is targeted, specific, and directed. That's positive, not negative. Think of it as being always in a problem-solving state of mind.

PATIENCE

It's said patience is a virtue, which is true. Unfortunately, it's something that's in incredibly short supply. We spend way too much time buzzing around in a "don't have enough time" frenzy, correcting things, redoing things, retrofitting, re-analyzing things after the fact.* Reacting rather than reflecting. There was a time when on being presented with a problem, managers would respond by saying, "Let's think about it. Let's mull it over and see if we can come up with a solution. Once we do that, we test it out. Does it solve the problem? If so, let's start production and marketing." This approach required planning and preparation. To be blunt, the planning and preparation stage is ceding more and more precious real estate to the production and deployment stage of product and service development. We are rushing into production and headlong into deployment with minimal lead times devoted to consequences. We are not taking the time necessary to properly consider why.

THE "CHASE IT DOWN" AND THE "WAIT PATIENTLY" MODELS

The cheetah is the fastest land-based predator alive. Its speed, obviously, is its greatest asset. Having spotted its prey, a cheetah will employ its speed to chase it down. It's a frighteningly energetic capture-and-kill strategy. However, speed is not always all that matters. By dodging and changing direction, its prey can evade the cheetah long enough for the cat to exhaust

---

* There is a big difference between merely "questioning" something (a product aspect, a process, a system, et cetera) and being in a constant state of curiosity. Questioning can arise from defensiveness; it can be a tool of criticism ("Are you sure this will work?"). Creativity, on the other hand, steps back from the table to get a broader (more objective) perspective ("I wonder if this might work.") In practice, the difference between the two approaches can appear vanishingly small and subtle, which is why it's so important that it's a mindset everyone understands and accepts.

itself. A cheetah's speed is inversely proportional to its endurance. It can run very fast but only for a short period of time.

The lion lacks the cheetah's speed and must instead pursue a predator in a stealthier fashion, hiding in the bushes or tall grass, observing, and planning, biding its time until the moment is right — for instance, when its prey has let down its guard and is drinking from a watering hole.

One approach is biased toward the impulsive, the other to the patient and methodical. Which is better depends a lot on circumstance (context). When speed is *all that matters*, the cheetah has an advantage. As we know, however, haste can backfire. When strategy is required — a plan — the lion prevails.

We are not taking the time necessary to properly consider why.

The contention in this chapter is that speed is never *all that matters*. There is a simple reason for speed limits: to minimize the severity of an accident. Too slow (being overly cautious) is just as bad. It's always about a balance; not short term versus long term. Both. When we say we will never stop asking why we are acknowledging the need to respond to short-term priorities while maintaining a focus on the long term ... the "what happens next?" and "what happens after that?"*

WHY AS A WAY TO FOCUS ON WHAT MATTERS

When a culture-driven leader says, "everything is up for discussion," they mean process, not goals and mission. Not culture. Means, not ends. In the right culture, why isn't about doubt or confusion; it's about achieving new perspectives, about exploration into and deeper thinking about how best to achieve the mission and establish alignments. Being thoughtful is not disruptive, but constructive. It's a form of self-discipline that is not easy to

---

* In fact, this chapter and the next are thematically equivalent. The culture-driven leader is never only a short-term leader but always has the "what's next?" and "what comes after this?" mindset. Always planning ahead and preparing. Always wondering how best to accomplish a task and moving on.

master. It takes time. We have become far more a reacting culture than a reflecting one. The room has become noisier and noisier; the pace of life is accelerated to such a degree that answers are demanded instantly.

Be efficient! Yes, absolutely! Time is an incredibly valuable (and increasingly rare) resource. It shouldn't be wasted. The paradox of improved efficiency is that it takes a huge investment of time and resources to achieve. What are we doing? Why this way? What about doing it another way? How could we do it more productively? Great questions, but most of us don't have the time to find out.

> **The paradox of improved efficiency is that it takes a huge investment of time and resources to achieve.**

A leader of course is focused on the necessary conventional metrics: profits, market share, share value, growth and productivity, et cetera. But how are all these being shaped and guided? Are you — is your mindset — in a leadership or a custodial role? It's an attitude and a mindset. I will argue that what characterizes the strong culture-driven leader is a commitment to constantly asking why. What are we in business to do? And how does that goal or mission instruct or inform how we do it? Can we do better? If so, how? If not, why not? It's a brand of thinking that values conservation where consistency matters (values and goals) but innovation and renovation (when timely) over mere preservation (when in a defensive position).*

PREPARATION AND PLANNING

Not one or the other: both! Of course, but how many of us really do the preparation and planning required for success? I can't tell you how many

---

* It's my experience that contemporary leadership often parrots the culture-driven model (employing slogans versus authenticity) but too seldom is guided by it; in other words, leadership is managerial (custodial) in behaviour. Intense pressure and competition, and decision-making timeframes that have shrunk to nothing, encourage this kind of behaviour. If you're always dealing with the here and now, it's harder to step away and look at the big picture.

times I have started fixing something in the bathroom, in the living room, or on the roof, and realized that I haven't brought along the right tools, or I have the wrong part. I tell myself I need to slow down and think more about what I'm doing. What's the process and have I mapped it all out the way I should? Chances are, no; it's just not the way we tend to do things.

It is absolutely essential to create the time necessary for preparation and planning. How much time? That is dependent entirely on how well you and the entire organization or enterprise understand and comprehend the goals and the mission. Not having the time required to *completely comprehend* what you are attempting to accomplish will negatively impact what you accomplish.

A common mistake is underestimating the time it takes to do things right. Our society is hard-wired to want immediate results. We send out an email and if we don't get a response in ten seconds we are puzzled. The increasing pressures and accelerated expectations of our globalized marketplace have made demand-side prioritization incredibly challenging. We talk so often about collapsed timeframes and increased competition and the need to "do it all faster." It can feel like an asteroid headed directly at you and your business. Without the focus on the why (embodied by the plan-and-prepare mindset) the risks of a direct hit expand exponentially.

TIMING: THE TOUGHEST "SELL" OF ALL

In the old days, company boards were made up of a dozen or so solid and sober-minded individuals who conceived of their role as providing cautious advice. Slow and steady, right? Remember the plodding tortoise in Aesop's cautionary tale about who wins the race? The tortoise, not the hare. Were Aesop around today, the tortoise would almost certainly have been fired by now — probably not even a quarter of the way into the race — and the company would already have been on its third or fourth CEO with the finish line still nowhere in site.

In the past, boards of directors tended to be risk averse: it was understood that profits were hard-earned and not to be gambled away. A company was a brick-and-mortar presence that had been built to endure. If you as

CEO floated a proposal that threatened to jump the guardrails and proceed in a new direction, the board would argue strenuously against it. It's very different today. I don't know how many conference tables I've sat at over the years, and for the most part, it's the hare's mindset that prevails.

Here's a typical scenario. You begin the board meeting with an agenda that — you admit frankly — includes some good news and bad. After all, it's your job, you assume, to inform the board and not sugar-coat the truth. "First, the good news." We hit this and that target. We exceeded quotas on so-and-so. And on it goes. All in all, a pretty great report.

> A common mistake is underestimating the time it takes to do things right.

"And now the bad news." A few members begin to nervously fidget. "We have a few issues and resolving them will require more time and certainly more investment. It's a short-term hit, and not ideal, I admit, but it will be a lot better for us in the long run." You look around the table. No one is happy, of course. The disappointment — the letdown — is palpable. "Look," you explain, "these are issues that could not be anticipated, and resolving them is absolutely essential if we want to stay ahead of our competition. But the problems will be fixed. We just need more time."

The frustration takes shape. "What's the real problem?" one of the board members asks impatiently. "Why was it not in the budget and plan?" "Why didn't we know about all this sooner?" On and on it goes until someone finally says it. "To be honest, we thought you had a grip on things. That's what you are known for. That's why we hired you. This doesn't sound like winning to us."

It doesn't matter how complicated the issues are, how difficult it might be to resolve, how important it was that the issues had been identified now as opposed to later when the consequences would have been disastrous. The responsibility rests with you. It doesn't matter what unexpected or contingent problems or complexities you are compelled to deal with. All that matters is that it isn't the answer they wanted (and expected). You rode in on the white horse! You were going to lead the troops up the mountain! The tenure of the average CEO, as we learned in an earlier chapter, is short.* The point is, you are still leading the troops up the hill … *just not today*. It's true, of course, that a board member isn't being paid to be patient; their job is to snap the whip. Same for a stake- or shareholder. *Win now, or else!*

Unfortunately, a leader doesn't have the luxury of acting impulsively or prematurely.

THE STRAIGHT LINE FROM A TO B

Complexity is real. It's a permanent feature of life and we need to deal with it — especially as leaders. After all, leaders are *by nature* expected to accomplish what is difficult to achieve. What an effective leader understands intuitively is that complexity (context) can't be legislated or voted out of existence. In other words, it may make one feel better to pretend a straight line from A to B exists, but it doesn't (or if it does, it only exists *for the moment*). It's not a new insight. Remember the example of Pompey from our first chapter? He unwisely caved to the peremptory demands of an impatient Senate and lost the battle with Caesar in a spectacularly humiliating fashion. It's an interesting question what might have happened had he trusted his instincts! Had he not impulsively changed tactics.

We need to pay attention to complexity and the dynamics of context.

Consider the following example: between August and November 2022, NASA's highly anticipated launch of its Artemis rocket — the most powerful in the world — was delayed four times (due to either weather or technical problems). "This is a massively complex vehicle," a NASA project manager explained. "It's the largest rocket we've ever built. And it has so many parts! Literally, millions of parts, and they all have to work. There are a lot of reasons launches get delayed."[1]

In fact, in the history of NASA's Shuttle program (135 missions) only 40 percent launched on time. It's why, the NASA manager said, they "test

---

* Paradoxically, a critical skills shortage (especially at the executive level) is forcing many companies to scramble to fill critical leadership roles. Executives are needed more than ever, in other words, but are facing shorter and shorter performance-related timeframes.

everything they can think of long before the rocket gets out onto the launch-pad for what [is called] a 'dress rehearsal.'"[2] When it comes to rockets blasting into space, chances are few people need to have complexity explained, nor do hordes of naysayers appear demanding immediate "changes at the top" when weather or technical issues scrub a launch.

The average leader in business, however, does not have the same luxury. The accelerated pace of modern life reminds me of the backseat passenger who is always barking out, "Are we there yet?" Doing something well takes time.

How hard is it to design a brand-new, consumer-friendly chequing account? It's not rocket science, after all. Well, yes, actually: *it is*. It's doubtful the average person appreciates the mind-boggling complexity of the average smartphone, but it's there. At the other end of the spectrum, the humble pencil is itself something of an engineering miracle. The point is, nothing is simple or easy; *it's just meant to seem that way*. And anyone who has ever been in a leadership position in just about any enterprise will come across challenging complexities in what might appear even the simplest task. It's for this reason especially that leaders of tomorrow need to embrace a why mindset. It's how we deal with complexity. And just as important, figuring out ways to sell complexity.

KNOW THYSELF

"Know thyself" was the maxim made famous by the philosopher Socrates more than two thousand years ago. It holds true today. Distilled to its essentials, this maxim simply underscores the importance of being aware of the why in whatever we think we know or do. Asking questions is the starting point for all students in whatever discipline, and the benefits of the Socratic method were reinforced for me when I became a professor with students of my own.

To be perfectly honest, it wasn't easy standing in front of an auditorium full of quizzical students asking why. However, it turned out to be an incredibly invigorating and creative experience. The alternative, students simply staring at me blank-faced or complacently taking notes, would have been incredibly disappointing.

We never stop being students; we should never stop asking why. If we're lucky, we can also serve as teachers, coaches, and mentors, doing whatever we can to help support others to build the habit of asking why, encouraging them and provoking new thoughts and new ideas. A leader who instills the questioning and inquisitive mindset in a culture and makes their actions align with that mindset sets up a winning culture and will get better results. It's never about fast; it's always about fast and right. Looking at things differently and searching for new opportunities is difficult. The goal will never be reached if only you adopt this mindset. Everyone in the organization needs to have really bought into it, and the culture needs to support it bottom to top. The unique challenge for the leader is acting quickly and effectively to make sure alignments are respected and sustained.

> We never stop being students; we should never stop asking why.

Asking why honours the process of posing the right question and solving for the right solution. It starts with engagement. Encouraging your team or employees to always be asking why is an investment they are making in the outcome. It turns a why into a very positive and directed why not.

WHAT'S YOUR MOTIVATION?

Unfortunately, most workers aren't engaged. In a recent Gallup "State of the Workplace" survey, only 15 percent of employees reported being "engaged" in the workplace.[3] An overwhelming number (85 percent) don't feel they have much of a stake in the jobs they do, probably aren't committed to the business's missions and values, aren't motivated, are mostly indifferent to its goals and outcomes, and don't really care that much about how well they do their jobs. A job is just what they do, and work is just the place where they do it.*

---

* The good news is that U.S. workers are about two times more likely (33 percent) to be engaged than their global counterparts. Still, that 67 percent of us are "not engaged" at work is hardly encouraging data.

Low employee engagement, according to the survey, costs U.S. companies $450 billion to $500 billion each year.[4] "Disengaged workers take less responsibility and ownership of their attitude, behavior, and motivation, and drain overall productivity."[5] Companies are encouraged to "focus on encouraging personal agency and … use tools to monitor and maintain personal engagement. It is also important to connect the employees' job to organizational missions, provide recognition and encourage collaboration." The Gallup survey reported that "the business or work units that scored the highest on employee engagement showed 21 percent higher levels of profitability than units in the lowest quartile. Companies with highly engaged workforces also scored 17 percent higher on productivity."

What should interest the culture-driven leader is that 73 percent of employees, according to Gallup, "would consider leaving their jobs for the right offer, even if they [weren't] looking for a job at the moment." Most interestingly, 23 percent of potential job seekers "wouldn't need a pay increase to take a new position."[6] Asking why is a head start on creating and sustaining value, for the customer, of course, but also for employees.

I have conducted hundreds of interviews with employees over the years, and for a not insignificant number, salary has not been the deciding issue. What employees want more than anything else is to be valued. Eighty-four percent "of highly engaged employees were recognized the last time they went above and beyond at work, compared to only 25 percent of actively disengaged employees."[7] In other words, "taking employees for granted is a sure-fire way to drop down the levels of employee engagement." Employees need to be made to feel "heard and valued." Being recognized — having it demonstrated that your contribution to the mission has value and is valued — "leads to increased motivation, a sense of pride and to increased self-confidence at work, which in turn increase employee initiatives and taking responsibility of one's own work."

> What we need to do as leaders is make sure we all have "our share of sunshine."

184

I used to tell my staff that what I wanted *them to feel* was what *I felt*: we were all on the same journey and one day we would look back at all this as being the best time of our lives. The "well-invested" promise, right? Yes, financial success is good, and I wanted everyone to enjoy their fair share. But it was more than that. What we need to do as leaders is make sure we all have "our share of sunshine."

FINDING THE RIGHT TOOL TO MAKE A DIFFERENCE

The famous Greek inventor and mathematician Archimedes supposedly said, "Give me a place to stand, and a lever long enough, and I will move the world." Archimedes had it right. Lifting an enormous weight, for instance, is made effortless if the problem is reconfigured. With the right lever and enough distance, nothing is too heavy. Give me a place to stand. Not just anyplace, Archimedes meant. You need to be in the right place. Taking the time and distance required to focus on the basics, to find the right place, is not just a fun exercise; it's an incredibly valuable tool for problem-solving and decision-making. But too often we stand firm. We don't find the right place to stand. We stubbornly cling to what we think we know. When that doesn't work, we double down.

Culture-driven leadership is about focusing on the basics and asking *the right* questions. Archimedes was wildly ambitious. He wanted to move the world. But there are many ways to move the world, some bigger than others. Just keep looking; that's the important thing. For instance, I didn't set out to revolutionize the retail banking market. It was more a case of the banking industry revolution finding me. True, I was always a why-asking person. Whatever the reason, once I started asking why I never stopped. I said I never fit in with the clubbish elitism of the banking industry, but it wasn't because I wasn't good enough. I knew I was. I was lucky enough, I think, to see that there was another way to do banking. I knew there were customers not being served by the conventional banking industry and simply wondered, "Why aren't they?"

I started riding a Harley because I couldn't afford a car. As a result, I was dubbed the "bad boy of banking" and then "rebel with a cause." For me, it just seemed a natural evolution from why to what became a revolution in retail banking.

THE BREAK/FIX MODEL

I just said that the key for effective leadership is creating a climate of curiosity; it's about asking the right questions. The questions we ask say a lot about how we define and value our priorities. Let's consider an example of a company that asked the wrong questions, and what happened as a result.

In a stretch of four months between late 2018 and early 2019, 346 people died in two crashes involving a Boeing 737 Max. At first, the crashes were blamed on pilot error. The real error, however, turned out to be a software glitch in its automated MCAS flight-stabilizing system that could cause the aircraft to unintentionally stall.

Boeing insisted it was not to blame. "Boeing has no higher priority than the safety of the flying public," it stated in a company release. After an investigation was conducted, Boeing would be forced to concede that, however, it *had known* about the software problem and had minimized the issue because of financial and competitive pressure. It seemed that Boeing had a culture that made "company deadlines a priority over passenger safety."[8]

When interviewed, 737 Max engineers described the company atmosphere at the time as an intense "pressure cooker." As a result of "extremely compressed" timelines, "rushed designers were delivering sloppy blueprints" to their bosses. An engineer was told "that the instructions … would be cleared up later in the process."[9] The break/fix model used to be the default for most problem solving; its genius was its simplicity: something breaks, no problem. We'll fix it. Unfortunately for the relatives and loved ones of the 346 passengers and crew who were killed, the "fix" arrived way too late.

It doesn't take a magic ball to see the potential in new products, services, and businesses. It's much harder to intuit and gauge the consequences of delivering those to the public, which is why effective culture-driven leadership is focused on making sure the consequences are understood as much as possible. No one said leadership was easy. Boeing leadership had *incredibly* difficult decisions to make. Billions of dollars and thousands of jobs were at stake. A decision they should never have made, however, was prioritizing profit over safety. It was a catastrophic example of failed leadership (and culture) to put one ahead of the other. The failure of culture that resulted in the Boeing 737 Max tragedies cannot be allowed to happen again. The stakes are simply too high. We need to do better.

What about taking risks to make money? All business involves taking a risk. But who should be taking the risk? According to U.S. automotive statistics, there were four hundred crashes over a ten-month period "involving vehicles with partially automated driver-assist systems," 70 percent of which were Teslas.[10] Is self-driving technology so vitally important that we are okay with human beings acting as beta testers? It seems ironic that a technology that could end up saving lives is today a threat to large numbers of lives.*

We know that software is routinely released to the public with known flaws. The companies releasing the software clearly believe that the flaws aren't crucial, and fixes can be patched in at a later date. The more important consideration is meeting delivery timeframes. *We could take three months to fix all the problems we know about, but by then our competitors will have had the jump on us.* (Of course, what this means is that developers — not consumers — are making crucial decisions about how quality is defined

> Culture-driven leadership is about focusing on the basics and asking *the right* questions.

and delivered.) What about the risks and flaws/glitches they don't know about? As I am finishing this chapter, Facebook and X are offering enhanced security packages to customers for a monthly fee. Why should customers have to pay extra for protection against vulnerable software? Shouldn't protecting your customer be a given? As one tech writer countered, "What would I pay for? How about a version of Facebook that completely respects my privacy."[11]

Yes! Why can't we do this? *It's what customers want.*

By the way, eleven people died in a four-month period in 2022 behind the wheels of cars equipped with autopilot systems. By comparison, since

---

* I am not aware that Elon Musk himself or anyone who works for Tesla currently drives a car with ADA (adaptive cruise control) technology, which reminds me of why so many social media pioneers dissuade their children from going online. When we can't predict risk, shouldn't we take the cautious "slow it down a bit" approach? Or is getting the newest product iteration to market ahead of the competition all that matters?

the space program originated in 1959 — *sixty-five years ago* — NASA has lost eighteen astronauts. As technology and the pace of innovation gain momentum in the years ahead, leaders will need to know its *true costs* and consequences. As we have seen already, many leaders don't.

A CEO SHORTAGE, BUT NO ANSWERS

As I write this, headlines are warning us that many of the country's largest retailers can't find the executive leadership they need. In 2022, for instance, "11 of the 91 retail companies in the Fortune 1000 saw chief executives leave."[12] According to a leading industry consultant, "The leadership challenges in retail right now are at an all-time high. There's a lot more questions about the right type of leader to navigate retail."[13]

Chief executives are being expected to "adapt to a retail landscape they weren't trained for and learn a wider array of skills to help their organizations navigate" a mostly unfamiliar and foreign terrain. "Top executives are also expected to understand how many resources should go to e-commerce operations compared with brick-and-mortar stores, how to troubleshoot issues in global supply chains and when to invest in emerging technologies like the metaverse."[14]

> What is the point of having more leaders if there is no culture to support them?

I don't know what the answer to the leadership challenge is, and I don't mean to undervalue just how important a bigger and more complete skill set will be for leaders of the future. It seems true to me, however, that the idea that "character is destiny" has a lot to recommend itself and should not be ignored. Skills are important, and so is experience. But effective leadership is a lot more than what can be gleaned from a resumé or an interview. What is the point of having more leaders if there is no culture to support them? What is the point of spending billions on a new generation of leaders only for them to inherit the same dysfunctional culture that created execution problems in the first place?

My experience years ago in Montreal still resonates with me. It was a reminder that I needed to keep pushing and working harder. I have used that experience in my own career, and when I hired people, I looked for the same burning desire. Yes, you have the skills. But do you have that something extra? For me, it always came down to character. Call it a chip on the shoulder, a cause, whatever. Are you open? Are you curious? Are you passionate about doing it better? If you are someone who has leadership potential, there are probably experiences you have already had that are signs of the leader within. When have you committed to a cause? How? What were the stakes?

You can't find that on a resumé.

IT'S ONLY GOING TO GET HARDER

Not long ago, I came across an interview with someone who was supposedly a management and leadership expert but had two of the most common misconceptions about the role of leadership. They believed that "being the boss means the boss makes all the decisions."* It isn't nearly as simple as that. If it were, life as a CEO really would be wonderfully straightforward. The truth is, CEOs don't have the authority and autonomy one might assume. In fact, it can often feel very much the opposite. The leader is always the one who is in the crosshairs. Part influencer, part decision maker, it's the leader who also carries all the final responsibility. Ultimately, it's your fault. No exceptions. When I say that 80 percent of my success has been the direct result of hiring the right people, I mean it! It doesn't matter how great you are as a leader. You have to have people around who can get it done. You can't do it alone! I always wanted managers to have some decision-making autonomy. If they were good at what they were doing, it only made sense. Obviously, the parameters of decision-making had to be appropriately defined and limited. Act inside your zone of expertise and all was good. I asked only that a bad decision be owned. Encouraging everyone to be curious about how we could do our best was a huge plus; it helps create investment from everyone in the mission.

---

* A concept made infamous in 2006 by President George W. Bush, who, rebuffing reports that subordinates were making key decisions, defined his role as president: "I'm the decider. I decide what's best."

According to the expert, the second key misconception is the assumption that "leadership is easy." *Hilarious.*

CONCLUDING THOUGHT

Creating a culture that values preparation and planning, that encourages and sustains reflection — committing to the principle that we will never stop asking why — is very difficult. It is also very time-consuming, which is why in our final chapter we will explore why it is so important for an effective culture-driven leader to have a "we are never finished" commitment.

ACTION POINTS

- Asking why is the door to seeing a problem and looking for an answer.
- Being aware of other possibilities energizes and helps to build buy-in for everyone.
- Reflecting is more important than reacting in leadership.
- An asteroid coming right at you is a priority. Leadership's task is also to *look beyond* the priority.
- Watch out for the shortcut that ends in a break/fix cost dilemma.
- It's not one person; it's everyone looking for answers together. A consensus of why gives everyone permission.
- If you don't ask why your customer will.
- Why puts as much emphasis on right as it does on fast.
- Question the leader, not leadership; question the means, not the ends.

Chapter 10

WE WILL NEVER BE FINISHED

As discussed briefly in the last chapter, the idea that "we will never be finished" is closely allied with the principle that we will never stop asking why. Together, they form a powerful cultural mindset that takes away the judgment of today in favour of one that focuses on the journey: tomorrow. And then another tomorrow. Instead of conceiving of every goal as a "finish line" crossed, it endorses development and continuity. No finish lines, just markers along the way. Life is a journey, and so is leadership. It requires a constant drive to do better and improve the quality of a mission and, in turn, life.

What any leader wants is for their leadership to endure. It's how you will be remembered. What your leadership will have meant. Unfortunately, leadership is always a work in progress. Not just for you, but for who comes after.

We will never be finished.

· · ·

Dante famously began his immortal work *The Inferno* with his disillusioned hero lamenting having found himself "In dark woods, / the right road lost." Nothing new in that insight! We all wonder at times where we're headed and why. Are we where we want to be? The daily conviction of the leader is to focus on people and culture — on the process and doing everything you can to create opportunities for everyone to invest in the journey. Your role is to actually make it a successful process and a successful journey. Yes, of course, results are important, but over time they aren't what matters.

"We will never be finished."

> **Culture-driven leaders see work as a journey without a clearly defined finish line.**

Culture-driven leaders see work as a journey without a clearly defined finish line rather than, as is conventional, something that focuses only on the here and now, only on the goals and targets set today to be realized by tomorrow. We all take pride in what we do; our ego and vanity convince us that it's all about us and our leadership. Then what? We all arrive someday at the point in the journey where we realize we have piled up a lot more yesterdays in our rear-view mirror than tomorrows that lie ahead. The road doesn't end; it just keeps going, mile after mile spooling out ahead of you. All you can do is think about the process and how you get there … that's what's important. Have the ends justified the means? Have you made the means themselves meaningful?

SIGNPOSTS AND MILESTONES

Everyday insights are no less profound for being common. The idea, for instance, that life is a journey, or that on that journey we constantly encounter a series of signposts, is not a new one. Dante found himself on the wrong road, right? We need our signs. How else do we know where we need to be going?

The problem is, we are conditioned from early on to adopt a task-focused start/finish mindset. So, we are *always* looking *only* for signposts and milestones. "Have you finished your dinner?" "Have you finished cleaning your room?" "Have you finished your homework?" We think everything will change when we graduate from high school, then it's college. *Yes, that's when everything will change.* Then it's the first job, the next promotion, the house, car, marriage, kids, the corner office, et cetera. One day, when you have all these things that were going to make all the difference, you start thinking about how much everything will change when you can finally stop doing what you have been doing and start doing all the things you always wanted to do.

"We will never be finished" is a way of giving you (and everyone who shares the journey) permission to keep improving. Keep getting better. Have you created a vibrant culture that can be passed on? I have been involved with seven startups in my career. Each time, I see the same signpost: Having done it once, can you do it again? Starting and staying with a project or a business is not easy, of course. On the other hand, the toughest thing is knowing when to stop, fold the tent, and move on. I have had to do that too. Stopping is heart-breaking, and the failure is always personal. No explanation of why it was necessary changes the disappointment. The mission, however, hasn't changed! Always be alert to new opportunities and fresh sources of inspiration. It's never over. As I have said before, if you ask any successful leader what they miss most, they will tell you it's not the money or prestige or the corner office. It will be the challenges, the energy, the people, the knowledge that they were on a worthwhile journey. That they were involved with something that mattered. Could they have done more? Can they do more? The trick is to always be looking; always be searching. Always be impatient with the status quo.

WHY THIS IS IMPORTANT: THE WORK–LIFE BALANCE

Most of us spend a lot more time at work than at home. How do we feel about it? Do most of us believe that we are on a workplace journey that we value and that we are valued as a part of that journey? If the data can be believed, no, we don't. Not at all. Consider:[1]

- Sixty-six percent of all full-time employees in the United States believe they have an unhealthy work-life balance.

- Sixty-nine percent of employees would love to have a more flexible work schedule, while 55 percent would prefer to work remotely.
- The latest work-life balance data shows that employees spend only 43 percent of their time on their primary job duties because they are required to be present at time-consuming meetings the rest of the time.
- Long hours lead to 27 percent of employees feeling depressed, 34 percent feeling anxious, and 58 percent feeling irritable.
- An estimated $125 billion to $190 billion are spent annually on treating the psychological and physical effects of burnout in the United States alone.
- Moral of the story: It isn't just you who wonders if you are on the right road. *Everyone does.* The leader's obligation is to be the vigilant and patient Virgil to your team's Dante: help them find the right road — and *keep on the right road*. It's the compelling attraction of principle-based culture. Goals might be short-term, but principles aren't. Tactics and strategy might be specific, not principles. They endure.

THE QUESTION OF CHARACTER

Who we are is always judged by what we do. Are our actions principle-based or transaction-based? Do we act based on rules or principles? Right or wrong? Good or bad? Do we cross any lines? No matter what we encounter, no matter what the context is, our principles should always guide our actions. People always see and judge a leader by their actions. Culture-driven leadership cannot be distinguished from character-driven leadership.

ARE YOU WHERE YOU WANT TO BE?

I have been involved in seven startups, as I said. Most have been very rewarding experiences, but not all. What made the difference? I soon found out: I didn't like my customers. It was that simple. I am from a working-class background, and the chip on my shoulder that has made me who I am has always been my identification with "the little guy." If that is not your audience, fine. But leaders are not one-size-fits-all types. Some lessons one has to learn more than once!

Do you like your customers? It's the "rubber meets the road" relationship in every business. If you end up embracing a principled-leadership style, the mission to improve lives, for instance, and to make a difference will be important. You can't be an effective teacher if you don't like students; or a good doctor if you don't like patients. I mean effective in a meaningful and memorable way. There are always exceptions, of course, but in leadership, as a rule, one's true feelings will filter through and will have consequences for the outcome.

> **Culture-driven leadership cannot be distinguished from character-driven leadership.**

I am very proud that more than half of ING Direct signups were women. The fact that so many women signed up with us validated my core belief that conventional banks had dropped the ball when it came to meeting customer needs. And helping to empower them made me work even harder. When it's only about the transaction — when I don't find myself passionately working on behalf of my customer — I lose interest. A leader doesn't have to be an advocate for their customer, but it sure helps. If customers believe you have their interests in mind, they will write you, come see you, talk about you, and impact your company's brand and your personal brand as well.

WILL YOU LIKE WHO YOU BECOME?

Leadership entails consequence, not just for your career but also for you on a personal level. It will change you, and right now you may not (probably don't) have any idea what those changes will be or who you will become. And you probably won't see the signpost until it's too late. Everything you do impacts your life. The longer you lead, the more it becomes who you are (and who you need to be). So, what are the consequences? What happens when you stop? I don't think there are a lot of leaders who have thought about this. It's the same situation as the actor who has played the same role to acclaim for so long that they can't remember a time when they weren't the character. Who are you without the role you play?

THE LEADER AS ÜBER ÜBER

You're the leader. It sounds great, until you realize that everyone expects you to deliver. Always and all the time. You are always placed out front and everyone is watching you as an example, role model, and inspiration. It's exhausting. And often frustrating. Followers are demanding. Employees are demanding and — as we have seen — their increased focus on work-life balance issues coupled with the demands for performance from boards of directors and stakeholders is putting even more pressure on leadership to *keep delivering*. It's not about what you want. You may think you're calling the shots and running the show, but it's never that simple. You're locked in a small room crowded with others, all telling you what you need to do and how you need to do it and blaming you for every mistake or stumble. You are always proving your value. Everything counts all the time. There are no time outs or off the record. Ever.

LEADERSHIP IS ALWAYS ABOUT PERSPECTIVE

Remember, you're the one at the front of the line. No one else sees what you see. Your job as leader is to create a consistent "here's what we see" cultural narrative that aligns with and reinforces goals and the mission. You need to stand apart. You need to lead others on the journey. For me, it always helped to remind myself that I am by nature an outsider, a rebel. What choice did I really have? Nothing will happen unless someone wants it to happen, right? Who will that someone be?

PERSEVERE

Hard work and dedication will make the dream become reality! Never give up! Persevere to see it through. The win is right around the corner. Knowing when to take on an opportunity, when to stay with it, and when to stop and close the chapter and find a new venture are classic leadership challenges that will be learned. We all face adversity in life, no exceptions. How you meet those challenges will determine how good a leader you are. It marks your reputation.

LEADERSHIP: IT'S LONELY AT THE TOP

I saved this entry for the last just because it can be the hardest for any leader to deal with: I call it the Judas moment of leadership. You will be betrayed. No use pretending it won't happen; it will. It's a crushing moment. It can easily undermine your confidence and make you doubt your self-worth and the value of everything you've worked for.

When I was CEO at Deak International, the company embarked on a corporate restructuring. I had been building the business for three years and was anxious to increase profitability and push ahead with business growth. The timing, however, was not good. I knew it, but I wasn't sure everyone agreed. In any case, dealing with lawyers, investment bankers, and accountants made for a very stressful three years.

A sudden board meeting was called, and when I walked into the conference room, I found my general counsel (and good friend) already there. I knew some-

You will be betrayed. No use pretending it won't happen; it will.

thing was wrong since no one was making eye contact and there was no small talk. The chairman began the meeting by questioning the wisdom of my latest decisions and actions. I provided an update. It didn't go well. "There were concerns," the chairman said, with the progress of my leadership. Did I think I was the right leader for the transition? I said yes. I asked if there had been a vote on a change of leadership. All this time, my good friend never took his eyes off the desk in front of him. They asked me to step out of the room. I left the room; he stayed behind. It confirmed my suspicion that he was my Judas. I was out as CEO; he was in.

I was devastated by the betrayal. It was gut-wrenching. I was shaken. I couldn't believe it. Why didn't I see this coming? Was I a complete failure? It's said it can be lonely at the top. Until you've been there, you have no idea.

Here's what I learned: there will always be a Judas in your inner circle. That isn't an insight. Any leader or CEO will tell you the same. And the probability is very high that it will be someone very close to you. What do you do?

This is the insight: *nothing*. You take the hit, repair the damage, and move on. You cannot be seen to be wasting time on a Judas moment. Don't fight it. Don't brood about it and second-guess yourself. "I should have known." "Why did I hire this person?" "What's wrong with me that I didn't see this coming?" And so on. It's a complete waste of time. Don't let it destroy you. Don't let it distract you. It is going to hurt, no question. It will damage you. Just walk on. Get back to what you need to do. You're still in the saddle!

Why is this so important? Because the quality of leadership — what will make it worth remembering — is if it *endures*.

THE NEED TO ENDURE: THE LEADERSHIP CHALLENGE

We are all familiar with the idea that in certain circumstances individuals "rise to the occasion." Often, we call these people heroes. That's nice, but not what we are talking about. Anyone can be a leader for an hour, a day, or even a year. If you have the stamina and the smarts and truly prevail — that is the real achievement. It's what really entitles you to be remembered. What is worth being remembered is leadership (leadership styles) that can not only survive but thrive over the long term, that remains even after a long series of changes of context.

We opened our story with a historical reference to the leadership styles of Caesar and Pompey. Consider that the first two emperors of Rome reigned for a total of sixty-six years. In fact, the first five emperors (the so-called Claudians) reigned a total of ninety-three years. By contrast, the nine emperors who reigned during the disintegration of the empire in the fifth century cumulatively lasted a mere fifteen or so years. One explanation: one group was focused on *exercising* power, another on *keeping hold* of power. Long-term commitment, in short, versus short-term. Of course, nothing endures in the long term if the demanding problems of the present are not dealt with effectively. Here's a really simple and common example: children only brush their teeth because parents insist on it. It's only years later, after it's a habit, that we understand and appreciate the value and benefits become obvious. Enduring leadership is like that.

CONCLUDING THOUGHT

Being an effective leader means finding ways to keep our commitments fresh and to honour our responsibilities and obligations. Keep making it better. It doesn't matter where you are on your path. Keep your eyes on the horizon. Keep looking for opportunities. Never put out the fire, stick to your principles. Never give up on a good idea; always be willing to adapt. And keep doing your best.

Years ago, I heard a (perhaps apocryphal) story about Ernest Hemingway. Whenever he was ready to finish for the day, he would make sure he stopped writing mid-sentence. That way he could quickly pick up his train of thought and keep going and wouldn't miss a beat.

The journey isn't over. It never is.

ACTION POINTS

- The definition of work is always changing.
- It's not about the work, it's about the journey.
- Every leader has a Judas moment; don't let it consume you or your mission.
- Leadership has a cost; it's the price you personally pay.
- For a leader the work-life balance will be weighted heavily toward work.
- It's never over, so never stop asking why.

Closing Thought

ABOVE THE CLOUDS – LEADERSHIP DRIVEN BY CULTURE

The leader is at the centre of any team, but they are always alone. To be in the thick of things and then find that the responsibility of being at the front and shouldering the decision-making is yours is not easy. You are on the ground as a leader making the aspects of the vision and the mission work. Goal-oriented and driven to get results.

I hope *Above the Clouds* has made the case that culture-driven leadership is the most effective and sustainable form of leadership. Not all cultures are the same, of course, but the underlying values and behaviours of a culture should, if aligned, underpin the ability to build teamwork and above all commitment.

For a leader, being observant, analytical, and focused is not enough. You have to get "above the clouds" to see the landscape in a broader and holistic way. But doing that is getting harder — the speed of change is accelerating; contexts keep changing. It's hard to read and see what works and what does not. We all are becoming harder to read and it's affecting our ability to work together. The more people involved, the more complicated it gets. *Exponentially.*

It reminds me of many personal experiences I have had in my leadership journey. After a long day of trying to make a situation work, struggling with issues, debates, and setbacks, I aways felt that we had not made any progress and that the project would likely fail. Exhausted, discouraged, even angry, my head spinning with details and data and endless things I needed to deal with, I'd head to the airport on my way to my next destination, and more discussions and expectations.

I was lucky; I had my "above the clouds" moment and it made a deep impression on me. I have never forgotten it. I found that adhering to the principles helped me maintain my inner equilibrium.

We can't do it alone. Sometimes we need someone on the ground — someone we truly trust — to be our "above the cloud" perspective. The person who can "tell it to us straight." It may not be what you want to hear, but you have to hear it.

But we're not always lucky enough to have a trusted ally we can depend on. As a leader you need to be your own best counsellor. Not the best cheerleader — the best critic. The trusted voice in your head that can allow you to view the situation from a removed or detached perspective. Wherever — or from whoever — you find it, you need to listen to your "above the clouds" voice.

FINDING THE RIGHT PERSPECTIVE

The "above the clouds" concept is not just about distance. It's finding exactly the right distance. What a culture-driven leader is looking for is the perspectival sweet spot. Leaders often talk about the value of short-term action and long-term thinking. What the culture-driven leader is searching for is the thinking that identifies and continually aligns both. Too much focus on the long term will result in the culture being undermined by context. Too much focus on the short term confuses context with culture.

I haven't heard too many people actually talking about perspective in the sense that they're too close or too far away. Listen to the average politician, for instance. What is being proposed might sound very nice. But will it actually solve the problem? Or is it simply a response to short-term priorities that will end up making the problem worse?

The key to being "above the clouds" is realizing it isn't simply about where you are. Getting further away from a problem isn't a solution unless it allows you to consider the problem from a more advantageous perspective. You can't be too low or too high. Leaders who find themselves consumed by the short-term perspective have what is called situational power (all about context). Leaders fixated on the long term have what might be called titular power (only about culture). A leader who can find the alignments between both has cultural power (a strong culture that recognizes context).

No matter how good you are, no matter how important you think your contribution has been, every leader eventually hits a finish line. If the culture is what it should be, the next leader can take over. It's as it should be. None of us ends up having as much time as we want; so, we have to make what time we have count. Every action you take, every opportunity met or missed, will become part of your legacy, not just as a leader but as a colleague, a mentor, a friend. Keep this book close. Nothing can be erased. Make it count!

AN "ABOVE THE CLOUDS" CHALLENGE

Try calling an 1-800 number. How was it? Over the years, endless amounts of money have been spent improving phone systems. Are things better? Were you impressed? Was it a positive customer experience? Probably not, because the improvements have been mostly supply-side driven. Not the culture-driven leadership approach. Try asking, "How could it have been better for the customer?"

What you may be experiencing right now is your first true leadership moment.

ACKNOWLEDGEMENTS

After living the experiences and sharing what I have learned in *The Orange Code* and *Rock Then Roll*, I could not stop thinking that so much more needed to be thought about and shared. It was in the midst of the pandemic that I realized leadership was changing in dramatic and fundamental ways. What I wondered was if (and how) the principles (and culture-driven leadership overall) had stayed the same or had changed. Have the leadership challenges and the context of today's environment changed? What had endured? What hadn't? Did we need something new? Or was what we needed a fresh update? *Above the Clouds* is the result.

It was my good fortune that I reconnected with Sam Hiyate and Jonathan Schmidt. Sam figured out how to get this book into the right hands, and I will always be indebted to Sam for his help and understanding. Jonathan walked with me through endless hours and drafts and debates on how the leadership perspective survives or dies in a culture big or small. Our debates and discussion not only got the job done, but helped build a friendship that made the task of writing a joy. I will always be grateful. I want to thank the wonderful crew at Dundurn Press who patiently and professionally guided the book from manuscript to finished book, especially Elena Radic, Laura Boyle, and Dominic Farrell.

Last, I want to thank my many colleagues and associates from ING Direct and Zenbanx: Jim Kelly, Tom Hugh, Scott Lugar, Rudy Wolfs, Kristi Walker, Mike Senechal, Frank Sanchez, Jim Joyce, Sadhana Akella-Mishra, John Young, Cleo Brown, John Bone, Todd Sandler, Eric Kuhlmann, John Owens, Cathy MacFarlane, Brian Myres, Daniela Bolkart, and Rick Perles. A few of the many! They are today distinguished alumni, great leaders in their own right, still fighting the good fight.

Appendix A

CULTURE-DRIVEN LEADERSHIP: A BRIEF PRIMER

Behind every successful leader is a vibrant culture that engages and energizes employees. In almost every case, that culture has been defined, shaped, and personified by the leader. The summary below describes the steps taken to build a distinctive, dynamic culture.

• • •

Business schools spend a lot of time training students to become leaders, teaching skills and increasing knowledge aimed at turning smart young people into effective leaders. Company training programs pick up where the schools leave off. Consider, for example, programs on workplace diversity, with their emphasis on communication and team-building. A critical component of team-building is culture, because if teams are to work effectively all employees must understand and embrace the culture of the particular group and business. There's no doubt that today, a leader's success depends on how they mould and develop that culture.

Shaping a culture is a formidable task, since many of the valuable qualities a leader might have are never taught in a classroom. They can be learned, but only from life experience. Emotional maturity, authenticity, and a strong character are all essential if leadership in a culture-driven company is to be effective. So is an alignment among the leader's passion, the company's mission, and the corporate culture in which everything transpires. But these characteristics are developed through life experience.

What are the steps we take to lead a culture-driven company? First, we'll examine the relationship between a successful leader and corporate culture. Next, we'll explore how to define a company's mission, which is central to visionary leadership. Finally, we'll lay out how to shape the culture you want at your organization.

LEADING THE CAUSE

Leadership folklore has always idolized the individual who is seen as larger than life. From the heroes of ancient Greece to the corporate raiders of the 1980s, we mythologize the chiefs who appear to be lone wolves or outsiders. Today, though, a new type of leadership is emerging — and it's just as effective as the old kind.

Today, it's possible to be in touch with anyone, anywhere, anytime. This development has had a profound impact on leadership. No single individual can be the central conduit for information about a particular company, because employees across the world are talking to colleagues and customers all the time. No one has all the answers, because the internet has given us instant access to experts on any subject. The old top-down leadership model has disappeared. The way we look at leaders has changed, and who we follow has become ever more situational. In fact, one of the reasons it seems so challenging to find successful political leaders today may be that the cultural dimensions of society have become too complex.

Globalization and social media have brought us vivid images of every scandal and embarrassment that embroils our leaders in the political, corporate, and entertainment realms. The result is that society has become more cynical and much less tolerant and admiring of leaders. That's not necessarily fair. Most leaders today genuinely try to get things done for good and even altruistic reasons. They are nonetheless often perceived as being driven by money, materialism, and self-interest. That perception is something leaders have to deal with, by redoubling their efforts to shake off the stigma of egocentric leadership and earn trust. No one is above it all. No leader can escape this reality.

To have an impact in this new environment, a leader must be closely aligned with the culture he or she hopes to lead. In the old days a culture might have been particular to one corporation, but that is unlikely today. Culture today must accommodate a much broader and diverse pool of employees, reflecting myriad languages, nationalities, genders, religions, ideologies, issues of work-life balance, and politics. The leader who parachutes in from the outside is a thing of the past. A leader whose own culture is inseparable from a company's culture is likely to be much more effective.

One popular concept of the corporation paints it as a money-making machine. But when employers and employees alike see the company this way, no one is very happy or productive. When everyone is just putting in hours for a paycheque, one has to ultimately ask, "What is the point?" Who gets what share of the profit? A successful company must have a cause that is bigger and broader than the organization itself. A successful leader must truly believe in a vision and a mission that can be combined to form a cause. He or she must be identified with the cause. "Walk the talk" is the most important criterion. The best leaders are those who derive their authority from having a genuine, inspiring sense of purpose.

An effective leader of a culture-driven organization will be recognizable by several traits. When others try to describe him or her, they think of the vision first. The leader is thought of more as a person devoted to a cause than as a manager running a company. They articulate and spread the values of the organization in a way that is explicit rather than implicit, and their personal commitment to success is obvious and frequently verbalized. The culture-driven leader constantly demonstrates passion and energy for the work to be done and is not alone in doing so. In a culture-driven company, the style of leadership itself is emulated at all levels of the company.

So, what type of individual is cut out to lead a company that is first defined by culture and a cause? They possess six fundamental attributes:

1. **A calling:** The leader must have a sense of purpose that is aligned with the company's vision. At ING Direct, for instance, our calling was to lead Americans back to saving.

2. **The guts to make the calling personal:** It must come from a real place. Otherwise, authenticity is missing, and no one sees the leader "walking the talk." The leader can't be an invention of the marketing department or the face of carefully scripted talking points. The leader has to be the author of the mission and feel a passion for it.

3. **A powerful enemy:** If there's no one to fight, there's no job for the white knight. Having a dark force against which to fight creates a highly effective leadership goal. The thought or image of an enemy transforms competitors into dragons to be slain by all employees. You believe that you are one of the "good guys." For workers, this makes coming to work every day more heroic and more of an adventure.

4. **An inner circle:** Picking a team is one of the leader's most fundamental responsibilities. Unfortunately, it's not easy to find and select people who would join a mission. The normal recruitment process does not work nor does the personal address book of colleagues. You network and search for the right people, many of whom are found in unusual places and circumstances. Character and motivation are the two qualities that separate loyal, enthusiastic workers from mere jobholders. Lots of people can put together good-looking curriculum vitae. Often, though, the best hire is someone who has experienced failure and has something to prove to themselves and the world.

5. **The possibility of failure:** Working in a constant state of imminent crisis is not for the faint of heart. It can, however, create a company-wide sense that the organization

(and everyone in it) is potential prey for an outside force. Without the risk of failure, everyone will grow complacent and corporate ego will become the silent killer. A sense of crisis keeps the enterprise in an energetic, startup frame of mind.

6. **An aura of mystery:** A leader can't make everything appear too mechanical. To drive the passion of your company, you have to create some mystery around you. You need to appear in some small, humble way as different from those that look to you. Team members want to follow, but they need a reason. It has to work like pixie dust.

THE MISSION

The most important question to ask about corporate culture is whether your team thinks they're in a job or on a mission. A visionary leader is on a mission, and inspires their employees to feel that way, too.

How do you begin to define the cause? It's a shame that the corporate mission statement went out of fashion, though it's easy to see why it happened. Too many such statements failed at their task. An effective vision has to be one that shakes up the status quo and starts a revolution. No one will ever be inspired by a puddle of ambiguity. Too many corporate mission statements were diluted into dullness by consensus and multiple levels of approval, making them utterly ineffective for rallying the troops. A mission statement, though, is the best leadership tool you can ever invent. In grassroots political organizations, the sense of being on a mission develops almost spontaneously, without central leadership, because enough people believe in the cause. A team with a purpose beats a team with a process any day.

So what makes the difference between a forgettable mission statement and one that turns workers into devotees? There are five key qualities to consider:

1. **A mission statement must advocate for someone:** At ING Direct, for instance, we set out to champion Americans who felt ostracized from and even preyed upon

by big banks; we had a different idea: we reached out to those customers. We're on your side.

2. **The goal in the mission statement should be nearly impossible to achieve:** Reaching for the goal — stretching — is the inspiring and satisfying part. It's a journey. The horizon should always remain just out of reach. We knew we couldn't turn everyone into a saver, but that didn't matter.

3. **A mission statement should read like poetry:** It should be sonorous and simple, and catchy enough that people won't be able to get it out of their heads.

4. **A mission statement should be written with the leader and the most loyal followers in mind:** It should not try to please everyone. It has to matter to the people who show up every day.

5. **The leader must come up with the mission statement themselves:** Defining the company's purpose is a leader's — and only a leader's — responsibility. Collaborating on its development or delegating the task goes against the very nature of visionary leadership. The leader must embody the company's cause and that includes being responsible for defining it.

GETTING THE CULTURE RIGHT

It is necessary to implement a feedback loop between the leader and the rest of the company as it grows. In a startup, the culture is a blank page in need of material. The leader must be aligned with the culture of the organization. At the same time, they must be responsible for shaping it. We created the culture through a set of bedrock principles we named the Orange Code. The code and the culture it created attracted new team members who shared the vision and the mission. A culture that is embraced by all becomes a more useful metric for measuring performance than traditional tools, and it keeps everyone engaged, committed to the mission and its outcomes. Skills matter, of course. As a company grows it becomes harder to ensure every hire is a cultural fit. A key to culture-driven leadership is learning how to measure both job performance and cultural behavior. As you can see in the graph below, an individual can fall into any one of four categories, plotted here along two axes. The vertical line measures job skills, while the horizontal line measures fidelity to the code, or culture.

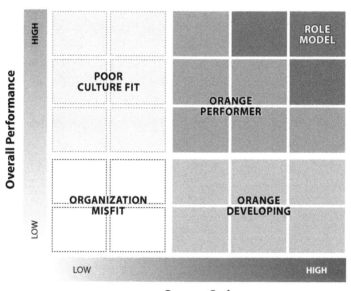

Source: Arkadi Kuhlmann, "Culture Driven Leadership," *Ivey Business Journal*, March/April 2010, The Ivey School of Business. Used with permission.

Someone with top-notch job skills who fully embodied the Orange Code would fall in the top right corner of the graph. These people were the role models for the rest of the organization. They were looked to as leaders. In practice we tended to look at culture first and job skills second. We found that someone who is a good cultural fit can learn and develop any missing job skills. The reverse is not true. Someone with great job skills but a poor cultural fit is unlikely to really embrace the code.

It is a fact that a corporate culture will be created with or without the involvement of the leader. But it is also a fact that creating and sustaining a *healthy* corporate culture requires constant attention and active involvement. Therefore, a leader should actively shape and direct the development of the culture.

Of course, a key part of shaping the culture is hiring the right people. It may sound counterintuitive, but I believe in hiring people who have made honest mistakes, because they most likely will have learned from them. We are all the products of our experiences, good and bad. However, successful people wish to remain successful, while others will do anything to become successful. The way we weather our storms shows true character.

Execution means being successful — getting it done. Six qualities define execution: accountability, empowerment, sense of urgency, customer advocacy, differentiation, and discipline. A leader who successfully executes will be seen, heard, and respected *as a leader*. For that to happen, you need the right team behind you, a team aligned with the culture you create.

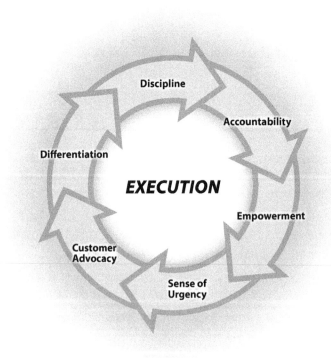

Source: Arkadi Kuhlmann, "Culture Driven Leadership," *Ivey Business Journal*, March/April 2010, The Ivey School of Business. Used with permission.

Even today, when I'm recruiting, I tend to look outside my comfort zone; what I am looking for are people with broad and unusual backgrounds. People who are too narrowly educated will make the right decisions some of the time, but they won't have the breadth of knowledge and experience to make the right decisions most of the time.

It's essential to try to understand the personality of the person working for you. Go beyond the slogans. It's the fireside chat versus the office chat. We team up for the right reason. We believe in the vision and will behave by the code that defines the company's culture. This is where a leader's true nature comes into play. If I am prepared to be completely open and honest with you, I am inviting you to be the same. That's the best chance I have as a leader to empower the culture of the organization and accomplish our mission.

NOTES

INTRODUCTION: WE NEED (BETTER) LEADERSHIP MORE THAN EVER

1   Andy Serwer, "What's Driving the Rise of 'Forever CEOs' — and Why It Matters to Investors," *Barron's*, June 23, 2023, barrons.com/articles/ceo-tenure-2023-57babe30?mod=Searchresults.

2   Danielle Abril, "Bosses Say Remote Work Kills Culture. These Companies Disagree," *Washington Post*, September 1, 2022, washingtonpost.com/technology/2022/09/01/remote-work-culture.

3   Mark Murray, "'Downhill,' 'Divisive': Americans Sour on Nation's Direction in New NBC News Poll," NBC News, January 23, 2022, nbcnews.com/politics/meet-the-press/downhill-divisive-americans-sour-nation-s-direction-new-nbc-news-n1287888.

4   Dominic Green, *The Religious Revolution: The Birth of Modern Spirituality, 1848–1898* (New York: Farrar, Straus and Giroux, 2022).

5   2022 Edelman Trust Barometer, edelman.com/trust/2022-trust-barometer.

6   Libby MacCarthy, "New Report Reveals 86% of U.S. Consumers Expect Companies to Act on Social, Environmental Issues," Sustainable Brands, May 18, 2017, sustainablebrands.com/read/marketing-and-comms/new-report-reveals-86-of-us-consumers-expect-companies-to-act-on-social-environmental-issues.

7   Felix Richter, "The Great Resignation Record: How Many Americans Left Their Jobs in November 2021?" World Economic Forum, January 18, 2022, weforum.org/agenda/2022/01/the-great-resignation-in-numbers-record/.

8   Ibid.
9   Paul Solman, "Hiring Slows in December as Worker Shortage Still Presents Challenges," *PBS NewsHour*, January 6, 2023, pbs.org/newshour/author/paul-solman.
10   Ibid.
11   Jose Ortega y Gasset.

OPENING THOUGHT: CULTURE VERSUS CONTEXT
1   All quotes from Simon Baker, *Ancient Rome: The Rise and Fall of an Empire* (London: BBC Books, 2006), 148.
2   Ibid.

CHAPTER 1: WE ARE NEW HERE
1   Helena Kelly and Tilly Armstrong, "How Sneaky Firms Hide Phone Numbers on Obscure Website Pages … to Stop You from Calling for Help: From BA, to Amazon and Barclays, We Put Them to the Test," *Daily Mail*, September 14, 2022, thisismoney.co.uk/money/news/article-11206439/How-sneaky-firms-hide-phone-numbers-stop-calling.html.
2   Katie Deighton, "Customer Experience Is Getting Worse," *Wall Street Journal*, June 7, 2022, wsj.com/articles/customer-experience-is-getting-worse-11654639388?mod=article_inline.
3   Ann-Marie Alcantara, "Customer Complaints, and Their Ways of Complaining, Are on the Rise," *Wall Street Journal*, June 14, 2020, wsj.com/articles/customer-complaints-and-their-ways-of-complaining-are-on-the-rise-11591998939?mod=article_inline.
4   Ibid.
5   Katie Deighton, "As Customer Problems Hit a Record High, More People Seek 'Revenge,'" *Wall Street Journal*, March 7, 2023, wsj.com/articles/as-customer-problems-hit-a-record-high-more-people-seek-revenge-2ab8fc74.
6   Ibid.

CHAPTER 2: WE ARE HERE TO CREATE, NOT DESTROY
1   Pete Evans, "And Just Like That, Peloton Shares Tank After Fatal Cameo in *Sex and the City* Reboot," CBC News, December 10, 2021, cbc.ca/news/business/peloton-shares-sex-and-city-1.6281652.

2 Ibid.

3 All quotes in this section are from Rob Copeland and Emily Flitter, "Goldman's Pitch to the Little Guy Turns Costly, as Struggles Mount," *New York Times*, January 13, 2023, nytimes.com/2023/01/13/business/goldman -sachs-david-solomon-ceo.html.

4 Ainsley Harris, "SoFi Edges into Banking with $100 Million Zenbanx Acquisition," *Fast Company*, February 1, 2017, fastcompany.com/3067811/sofi -edges-into-banking-with-100-million-zenbanx-acquisition.

5 David Gelles, "How Jack Welch's Reign at G.E. Gave Us Elon Musk's Twitter Feed," *New York Times*, May 21, 2022, nytimes.com/2022/05/21/business /jack-welch-ge-ceo-behavior.html.

CHAPTER 3: WE WILL CONSTANTLY LEARN

1 Oliver Staley, "How the Average Age of CEOs and CFOs Has Changed Since 2012," Quartz, September 11, 2017, qz.com/1074326/how-the-average-age-of -ceos-and-cf0s-has-changed-since-2012/.

2 Ibid.

3 Chad Brooks, "Time to Go? How Long Is Too Long for CEO Tenure?" Fox Business, December 24, 2013, foxbusiness.com/features/time-to-go-how-long -is-too-long-for-ceo-tenure.

4 Ibid.

5 Ibid.

6 Maya King and Jonathan Weisman, "Young Voters Are Fed Up with Their (Much) Older Leaders," *New York Times*, July 14, 2022, nytimes.com /2022/07/14/us/politics/youth-voters-midterms-polling.html.

7 Wyndham Lewis, *Time and Western Man* (Boston: Black Sparrow Press, 1993), xii.

8 Herb Greenberg, "Worst CEOs of 2011," CNBC, December 14, 2011, cnbc.com /2011/12/14/worst-ceos-of-2011-greenberg.html.

9 Neil Franklin, "Workers Worldwide Think They Could Outperform Their Own Bosses," Workplace Insight, September 10, 2019, workplaceinsight.net /workers-worldwide-think-they-could-outperform-their-own-bosses.

10 "Emotional Intelligence," Harvard Health Publishing, Harvard Medical School, 2020, health.harvard.edu/mind-and-mood/emotional -intelligence#about-report.

11 Ibid.

12 Melinda Fouts, "The Value of Emotional Intelligence for Leaders," *Forbes*, June 3, 2019, forbes.com/sites/forbescoachescouncil/2019/06/03/the-value-of-emotional-intelligence-for-leaders/?sh=36cc700d156d.

13 Ibid.

CHAPTER 4: WE WILL LISTEN; WE WILL SIMPLIFY

1   Andreas Kluth, "Science Shows Why Simplifying Is Hard and Complicating Is Easy," Bloomberg, April 24, 2021, bloomberg.com/opinion/articles/2021-04-24/research-shows-why-simplifying-is-hard-and-complicating-is-easy

2   William Arruda, "What Employees Really Think About Their Bosses," *Forbes*, December 12, 2017, forbes.com/sites/williamarruda/2017/12/12/what-employees-really-think-about-their-boss/?sh=1309efa1a1ec.

3   Pavel Krapivin, "Sir Richard Branson's Five Billion Reasons to Make Your Employees and Candidates Happy," *Forbes*, July 9, 2018, forbes.com/sites/pavelkrapivin/2018/07/09/sir-richard-bransons-5-billion-reasons-to-make-your-employees-candidates-happy/?sh=191e3f4b6710.

4   Greg Jaffe, "Starbucks CEO Howard Schultz's Fight to Stop a Starbucks Barista Uprising," *Washington Post*, October 8, 2022, washingtonpost.com/business/2022/10/08/starbucks-union-ceo-howard-schultz/.

5   Ibid.

6   Ibid.

7   Ibid.

8   Ibid.

9   Jonny Thomson, "Too Much Choice: The Strange Phenomenon of 'Analysis Paralysis,'" Big Think, May 19, 2022, bigthink.com/thinking/choice-analysis-paralysis/.

10 Morgan Mandriota, "Overwhelmed? These 9 Strategies May Help," PsychCentral, November 16, 2021, psychcentral.com/stress/how-to-deal-with-feeling-overwhelmed.

CHAPTER 5: WE WILL BE FAIR

1   Len Testa, "Bob Chapek Didn't Believe in Disney Magic," *New York Times*, November 29, 2022, nytimes.com/2022/11/29/opinion/disney-robert-iger-bob-chapek.html.

2   Ibid.

3   Oliver Darcy, "Bob Iger Moves Fast to Dismantle Chapek's Reorganization of Disney," CNN, November 21, 2022, cnn.com/2022/11/21/media/bob-iger-bob-chapek-disney-reliable-sources/index.html.

4   "Google to Pay $40 Million in Location Data Harvesting Suit," PIRG, May 22, 2023, pirg.org/updates/google-to-pay-40-million-in-location-data-harvesting-suit/.

5   Elizabeth Spiers, "This Is What Happens When Tech Executives Start Believing Their Own Hype," *New York Times*, June 28, 2022, nytimes.com/2022/06/28/opinion/kraken-powell-tech-culture-libertarianism.html.

6   Ibid.

CHAPTER 6: WE WILL TELL THE TRUTH

1   Elizabeth Dwoskin and Faiz Siddiqui, "Elon Musk Plans Twitter Layoffs with New Team," *Washington Post*, October 31, 2022, washingtonpost.com/technology/2022/10/31/elon-musk-twitter-layoffs/.

2   Elizabeth Spiers, "Layoffs by Email Show What Employers Really Think of Their Workers," *New York Times*, January 29, 2023, nytimes.com/2023/01/29/opinion/mass-tech-layoffs-email-google.html.

3   Geoffrey A. Fowler, "Electronics Are Built with Death Dates. Let's Not Keep Them a Secret," *Washington Post*, August 2, 2022, washingtonpost.com/technology/2022/08/02/why-gadgets-die/.

4   Steve Morgan, "Is Poor Software Development the Biggest Cyber Threat?" CSO, September 2, 2015, csoonline.com/article/2978858/is-poor-software-development-the-biggest-cyber-threat.html.

5   Aimee O'Driscoll, "Cybersecurity Vulnerability Statistics and Facts (2019–2024)," Comparitech, January 17, 2024, comparitech.com/blog/information-security/cybersecurity-vulnerability-statistics/.

6   Kevin Collier, "U.S. Warns New Software Flaw Leaves Millions of Computers Vulnerable," NBC News, December 14, 2021, nbcnews.com/tech/security/us-warns-new-software-flaw-leaves-millions-computers-vulnerable-rcna8693.

7   John Glenday, "Just Over a Third of Consumers Trust Brands, Say Clear Channel and JCDecaux," The Drum, March 24, 2021, thedrum.com/news/2021/03/24/just-over-third-consumers-trust-brands-say-clear-channel-and-jcdecaux.

8   Ivana V., "Job Satisfaction Statistics: Keep Your Workers Happy and Your Business Healthy," Smallbizgenius, June 17, 2023, smallbizgenius.net/by-the-numbers/job-satisfaction-statistics/.

9   Vibhas Ratanjee, "How to Build Trust in the Workplace," Gallup, June 14,

2022, gallup.com/workplace/393401/trust-decline-rebuild.aspx.

10 Ivana V., "Job Satisfaction."

11 Ibid.

12 "Why Brand Trust Is So Important," Dusted, September 8, 2023, dusted.com /insights/why-brand-trust-is-so-important.

13 Ibid.

14 Ryan Pendell, "CEOs: "Do Your Employees Trust You?" Gallup, June 7, 2017, news.gallup.com/opinion/gallup/211793/ceos-employees-trust.aspx.

15 2022 Edelman Trust Barometer.

16 Ibid.

17 Jed Perl, *Authority and Freedom: A Defense of the Arts* (New York: Knopf, 2022), 67.

18 "The Trust 10," 2022 Edelman Trust Barometer, edelman.com/sites/g/files /aatuss191/files/2022-01/Trust%2022_Top10.pdf.

19 Ratanjee, "How to Build Trust."

CHAPTER 7: WE WILL BE FOR EVERYONE

1 Associated Press, "Southwest to Add 4th Fare Level to Increase Revenue," Fox 40, March 25, 2022, fox40.com/news/national-and-world-news/southwest -to-add-4th-fare-level-to-increase-revenue/.

2 Ibid.

3 Krapivin, "Sir Richard Branson's Five Billion Reasons."

4 Ibid.

5 Ibid.

6 Rhianna Schmunk, "As Cost of Living Soars, Millions of Canadians Are Turning to Food Banks," CBC News, October 25, 2023, cbc.ca/news/canada /food-bank-use-highest-in-canadian-history-hunger-count-2023-report-1.7006464.

7 "Canada's Tech Sector Fuels Growth Across the Economy: BDC Study," BDC, January 31, 2022, bdc.ca/en/about/mediaroom/news-releases/canada -tech-sector-fuels-growth-across-economy.

8 "The American Middle Class Is Losing Ground," Pew Research Center, December 9, 2015, pewresearch.org/social-trends/2015/12/09/the-american -middle-class-is-losing-ground/.

9 Victoria Guida and Eleanor Mueller, "Stock Plunge Shakes Confidence of Higher-Income Americans," Politico, June 13, 2022, politico.com/news /2022/06/13/wealthier-americans-inflation-stocks-00039157.

CHAPTER 8: OUR MISSION IS TO HELP IMPROVE LIVES

1   Kristin Conard, "The Real Reason Tech Moguls Don't Let Their Kids on Social Media," The List, December 6, 2021, thelist.com/677684/the-real-reason-tech-moguls-dont-let-their-kids-on-social-media/.

2   Ibid.

3   "Customers Expect the Brands They Support to be Socially Responsible," Business Wire, October 2, 2019, businesswire.com/news/home/20191002005697/en/Consumers-Expect-the-Brands-they-Support-to-be-Socially-ResponsibleLeadership.

4   Udemy, "2017 Skills Gap Report," Udemy, research.udemy.com/wp-content/uploads/2017/11/Skills-Gap-Report-2017-2021-Rebrand-v3-gs.pdf.

5   Shayna Joubert, "Top 6 Leadership Skills for the Workplace of Tomorrow," Northeastern University, September 4, 2019, northeastern.edu/graduate/blog/essential-leadership-skills-for-tomorrow/.

6   Federica Laricchia, "Smartphones in the U.S. — Statistics and Facts," Statista, February 23, 2024, statista.com/topics/2711/us-smartphone-market/.

7   Sareena Dayaram, "Getting a New iPhone Every 2 Years Makes Less Sense Than Ever," CNET, November 22, 2021, cnet.com/tech/mobile/getting-a-new-iphone-every-2-years-is-making-less-sense-than-ever/.

8   Ibid.

9   Rani Molla, "Smartphones Are Getting More Expensive Around the World," Vox, October 24, 2017, vox.com/2017/10/24/16527600/smartphone-price-around-the-world-apple-samsung-huawei.

10 Katie Collins, "Billions of People Globally Still Can't Afford Smartphones. That's a Major Problem," CNET, August 5, 2020, cnet.com/tech/mobile/billions-of-people-globally-still-cant-afford-smartphones-thats-a-major-problem/.

11 Ibid.

12 Ken Sweet, "Capital One's Bid for Discover Carries Expectation That Americans Won't Slow Credit Card Use," Associated Press, February 24, 2024, apnews.com/article/capital-one-discover-credit-card-visa-merger-2264ec3d43143d06a1f6820d1241b033.

13 Ibid.

14 Ibid.

15 Ibid.

16 Cade Metz and Gregory Schmidt, "Elon Musk and Others Call for Pause on A.I., Citing 'Profound Risks to Society,'" New York Times, March 29, 2023, nytimes.com/2023/03/29/technology/ai-artificial-intelligence-musk-risks.html.

17 Ibid.

18 Terry Nguyen, "Consumers Don't Care About Corporate Solidarity. They Want Donations," Vox, June 3, 2020, vox.com/the-goods/2020/6/3/21279292 /blackouttuesday-brands-solidarity-donations.

19 Taylor Tepper, "Milton Friedman on the Social Responsibility of Business, 50 Years Later," *Forbes*, June 16, 2020, forbes.com/advisor/investing/milton -friedman-social-responsibility-of-business/.

20 Rebecca Jennings, "Why You're Getting Coronavirus Emails from Every Brand You've Ever Interacted With," Vox, March 24, 2020, vox.com/the-goods /2020/3/24/21192837/coronavirus-brand-emails.

21 Felix Salmon, "Corporations Pledge over $450 Million in Donations for Social Justice," Axios, June 11, 2020, axios.com/2020/06/11/corporations-charity -social-justice-donations.

22 James B. Stewart and Nicholas Kulish, "Leading Foundations Pledge to Give More, Hoping to Upend Philanthropy," *New York Times*, June 10, 2020, nytimes.com/2020/06/10/business/ford-foundation-bonds-coronavirus .html?stream=business.

23 Salmon, "Corporations Pledge over $450 Million."

CHAPTER 9: WE WILL NEVER STOP ASKING WHY

1   Jason Bittel, "NASA's Artemis I Launch Has Faced Several Delays. That's Actually Common," *Washington Post*, November 15, 2022, washingtonpost.com /kidspost/2022/11/15/nasa-launches-often-delayed/.

2   Michael Dodge, "Artemis Delay Is the Latest of Many NASA Scrubs and Comes from Hard Lessons on Crew Safety," PhysOrg, November 14, 2022, phys.org/news/2022-11-artemis-delay-latest-nasa-hard.html.

3   Valene Jouany and Mia Makipaa, "10 Employee Engagement Statistics You Need to Know in 2024," Haiilo, January 13, 2024, haiilo.com/blog /employee-engagement-8-statistics-you-need-to-know/.

4   Jouany and Makipaa, "10 Employee Engagement Statistics."

5   Ibid.

6   Ibid.

7   Ibid.

8   Natalie Kitroeff and David Gelles, "Before Deadly Crashes, Boeing Pushed for Law That Undercut Oversight," *New York Times*, October 27, 2019, nytimes.com/2019/10/27/business/boeing-737-max-crashes.html.

9   Ibid.

10   Tom Krisher, "U.S. Report: Nearly 400 Crashes of Automated Tech Vehicles," AP, June 15, 2022, apnews.com/article/self-driving-car-crash-data -ae87cadec79966a9ba56e99b4110b8d6.

11   Geoffrey A. Fowler, "Facebook's New $12 Fee Is Straight Out of Don Corleone's Playbook," *Washington Post*, February 23, 2023, washingtonpost.com /technology/2023/02/23/facebook-instagram-fee/.

12   Jordyn Holman, "The Retail C.E.O. Pipeline Is Running Dry," *New York Times*, February 16, 2023, nytimes.com/2023/02/16/business/retail -executives.html.

13   Ibid.

14   Ibid.

CHAPTER 10: WE WILL NEVER BE FINISHED

1   "Work-Life Balance Statistics [2023 Edition]," What to Become, May 16, 2023, whattobecome.com/blog/work-life-balance-stats/.

ABOUT THE AUTHOR

Dubbed a "rebel with a cause" and the "bad boy of banking," Arkadi Kuhlmann is among a handful of successful CEOs and entrepreneurs who truly have made a lasting mark on leadership. Kuhlmann began his career as a business professor, served as a banking industry consultant and then as vice president of Royal Bank of Canada. Arkadi revolutionized banking when he founded ING DIRECT, and as president and CEO turned it into the largest savings bank and the number one direct bank in the U.S., with eight million customers and more than $96 billion in deposits.

Kuhlmann is a dual U.S.–Canadian citizen, businessman, speaker, author, and artist. In July 2012, he founded his sixth banking startup, Zenbanx, serving as its CEO before its sale in 2017. Kuhlmann returned as CEO of a revived global Zenbanx in 2023.